BOOKS BY SABRA HOLBROOK

*The French Founders of North America and Their Heritage*
*Lafayette: Man in the Middle*

# Lafayette

*Man in the Middle*

Lafayette as Commander of the National Guard.
*Courtesy of the Lafayette Memorial Foundation.*

Sabra Holbrook

# Lafayette

## *Man in the Middle*

ILLUSTRATED WITH OLD PRINTS

AND PHOTOGRAPHS

*Atheneum   New York*

*1977*

*For another liberal aristocrat*

SIR JOHN INVICTUS BUFORD

LIBRARY OF CONGRESS CATALOGING IN PUBLICATION DATA

Holbrook, Sabra.
Lafayette, man in the middle.

Bibliography: p. 207
Includes index.
SUMMARY: A biography of the Frenchman whose belief in democracy led him
to participate in the American and French Revolutions.
1. Lafayette, Marie Joseph Paul Yves Roch Gilbert du Motier, marquis de,
1757–1834—Juvenile literature.   2. Statesmen—France—Biography—
Juvenile literature.
[1. Lafayette, Marie Joseph Paul Yves Roch Gilbert du Motier,
marquis de, 1757–1834.   2. Statesmen].   I. Title.
DC146.L2H563   944.04'092'4   [B]   77-2553
ISBN 0-689-30585-0

Published simultaneously in Canada by
McClelland & Stewart, Ltd.
Manufactured in the United States of America by
Halliday Lithograph Corporation
West Hanover, Massachusetts
*Designed by Mary M. Ahern*
First Edition

# ACKNOWLEDGMENTS

THE author would like gratefully to acknowledge the courteous and informed assistance given her at Chavaniac by the Administrator of the Lafayette Memorial Foundation, Monsieur Maurice Durand; also the gracious hospitality proffered by Madame Durand.

Thanks are also due to Monsieur Henri Léouzon and Madame Suzanne Léouzon of the Délégation Régionale du Commissariat General au Tourisme in Clermont-Ferrand, to George L. Hern, Jr. of the French Government Tourist Office in New York and to the Paris Headquarters of that agency for assistance with introductions. Karen Johnson of the Service de Presse et d'Information of the French Embassy was also most helpful with documentation.

# CONTENTS

# Lafayette
## *Man in the Middle*

# 1

## PRELUDE

### *Auvergne & Paris*

"I'LL have her thighs," threatens a man wearing the red, white, and blue stocking cap of the French revolutionist of 1789.

"I'll fricassee her liver," shrieks a woman.

They are mentally dissecting Marie Antoinette, the queen, wife of Louis XVI, King of France.

Along with a mob of some three thousand citizens, they have marched ten miles from Paris to storm the Palace of Versailles, the royal residence. The men in the crowd are disguised as women. During the riots which have been erupting for three months, the king has ordered the military not to fire on women. The men count on their masquerade to insure safe access to the courtyard.

It is October and cold. A mean mizzle of rain has soaked the protesters' clothing. Once inside the gates, the men shed their skirts, heavy with wetness. The women wring theirs.

But the spirits of none, though they have marched through the night, are dampened. They will have this haughty queen, this Austrian-born upstart, who with her disdainful ways is sometimes even more than her husband the symbol of what they seek to overthrow: the inherited power of the noble-born few to determine the fate of the common thousands.

The National Guard and the king's personal guards ring the palace. But the soldiers make only halfhearted attempts to break up the mob. So many of them sympathize with mob sentiment that the men's disguise was probably unnecessary. The Commander of the National Guard is already inside the palace. Reluctantly, he had accompanied the march from Paris. In no uncertain terms, its organizers, some of his own troops among them, had made clear that his choice was Versailles or the lamp post. He could march with them or be strung up.

The commander himself is a revolutionist, despite his aristocratic birth. "I am persuaded that the human race was created to be free and that I was born to serve that cause," he insists. But his idea of service differs from the mob's. Mob rule is as hateful to him as unrestricted royal rule. He wants justice—equal justice for all.

Therefore he is resolved that this mob shall not take over. At 5:00 A.M. he knocks on the door of the queen's chambers, awakening her. "Come with me and show yourself to the people," he demands. He leads her, protesting, a robe thrown over her nightgown, to a balcony outside.

A guttural roar rises from the crowd. "Do not shrink, Madame," he warns. Then bowing low, he kisses her hand.

The mob hushes at the sight. Though he had proved difficult about joining the march on Versailles, General Marie Joseph Paul Yves Roch Gilbert du Motier, Marquis de Lafayette, is a man in whose leadership the people place faith and hope. Never mind that he is not of them. He is for them.

They murmur. The murmur ripples, swells to a shout. But not an angry one. *"Vive le général! Vive la reine!"* Long live the general! Long live the queen! For this day at least, October 5, 1789, Lafayette's belief in orderly change had conquered the undisciplined impulses of a people blindly seeking to work out their own destiny.

Fayettism, as the philosophy that triumphed that day came to be known in France, was born of two intermingling currents in Lafayette's life. One was a devoted love of his own twelve-hundred-year-old nation, the other an equally devoted love of the world's newest nation in his time, the United States of America.

This man of two countries, this moderate liberal, came from the mountains of Auvergne, in the heart of France. In his ancestral, fourteenth-century chateau at Chavaniac, the window of the round tower room where he was born in 1757 framed a rugged view. The grown Lafayette made the room his study and placed his desk directly in front of the window. On clear days he could look northward toward the high place where the rivers of France divide, some winding west to the Atlantic, others rushing south to the Mediterranean. He could glimpse the colossal Puy de Sancy, jutting almost six thousand feet into the sky and dwarfing the other glacier-rounded summits in the volcanic spine of France, the Massif Central. In later years, he credited to the good fortune of having grown up among these mountains, both the impulsiveness which characterized some of his actions, and the fortitude with which he was able to endure hardships. "In my blood is the hot lava, in my bones the solid granite which formed the homeland of my youth," he wrote in his memoirs. And in spite of his love for America: "The whole New World would . . . not make me renounce that part of the old one where I had the good fortune to be born . . . an Auvergnat."

In the hilltop village which bordered the family chateau lived forty families. Lafayette knew them all, these villagers.

In the vaulted basement kitchen of the chateau they some-times gathered to roast a couple of sheep in a fireplace so big a half-dozen men could have stood in it. Bread would be baking too, made of grain harvested from the chateau's fields.

The young Lafayette was a welcome guest at these feasts. The villagers made much of him. He was not a handsome boy, their lord, despite the fineness of his features; the cres-cent eyebrows, the triangular nose, the exceptionally large, hazel eyes that lighted with interest at all that he saw, and the bowed lips that gave the impression of a permanent smile. His red hair, when not covered with the customary white wig of the times, always attracted attention, but be-neath it his face seemed misangled; it slanted inward, bottom to top. His narrow chin jutted out; his broad forehead re-ceded. He was tall and well-built, but neither as child nor man did he seem to know what to do with his arms and legs. His awkwardness became a joke. Introduced to court life in his teens, he was singled out by Marie Antoinette as a dancing partner. He stumbled so badly that the queen burst out laughing—and all the court with her.

Lafayette never forgot the ridicule. It helped form his dis-taste for the frivolities and formalities of eighteenth-century court life.

With the villagers of Chavaniac, on the other hand, he felt easy and comfortable. From them he acquired an under-standing of farm management and a love of raising cattle and crops which was balm to his soul between tense years in which he served revolutionary causes in the United States and France. Also, in the chatter-filled kitchen of the chateau he gleaned his first inklings of every man's need to be his own man. His association with the sturdy Auvergnats gave him the earliest roots of his faith in the collective wisdom of com-mon men.

The association began early in his orphaned life. His father was a military man who came from a long line of offi-cers. One had been a Marshal of France and companion-at-arms of Joan of Arc. When Lafayette was only two, his father was killed, fighting the English in a war touched off by conflicting colonial interests of France and England in North America and India. Technically lord of the manor, Lafayette was brought up by his mother, who died when he was thirteen. Two weeks later his grandfather died. Lafayette inherited his mother's chateau and his grandfather's fortune.

The manor house, rambling and roomy, was sunlit from one angle or another all day long. In almost every room there was a cheerful hearth; the larger rooms had two. There were intimate dining rooms for family, chandeliered dining rooms for formal occasions. There was a room for billiards and an inviting living room, decorated in comfortable country style. Outside, farmed fields, pastureland, vegetable gardens, orchards and vineyards stretched past a fishpond toward the mountains, and every chateau window opened on a different perspective of these. It should have been a happy home, but the atmosphere was depressing. Except for Lafayette—and briefly a young cousin—the inhabitants were women in black, three of them widows including his mother, the fourth a spinster. Lafayette's escape to the kitchen, his trips on horseback or on foot to granary and mill, fields and fishpond must have been, despite his dutiful attachment to his relatives, like sparks in the gloom.

His education didn't offer the same relief. At first privately tutored by his parish priest, he was sent at eleven to live with his grandfather in Paris, while attending the College du Plessis, a plush secondary school. He barely managed to graduate, his problem being that he detested reading. It was obvious, however, that his dislike of books and his poor scholastic record were no reflection of his true ability. An uncle, the Marquis François-Claude Amour, observed that he was "astoundingly advanced in the ability to reason . . . his thinking and perceptiveness are extraordinary. . . . This child has the kind of mind that belongs to great men."

Having edged through the College de Plessis, he went on

to military academy at Versailles, becoming a cadet in his grandfather's old regiment, the Black Musketeers. At sixteen he married the girl his guardian and her family had agreed upon, fourteen-year-old Adrienne de Noailles. There had been some question at first as to whether Adrienne or her sister Louise should be chosen. The question was answered when Louise was abruptly cloistered in a convent to escape the sexual advances of the French king, Louis XV.

Like Lafayette, Adrienne came from a military background; her grandfather, the Duke of Noailles, had been a Marshal of France. The marriage was arranged in the manner of the times; two socially equal families were profitably united. Adrienne's dowry was settled. Lafayette's proposed wedding gift to her—a basket of jewels and money—was found acceptable. In only one respect did the formalities differ from the norm. With unusual regard for the pair who were to form the union, Adrienne's mother invited the groom-to-be to live with the de Noailles for two years before the agreement went into effect. The board was not free—he paid the equivalent of $2000 a year for his keep—but the arrangement did allow the two children to become friends before becoming man and wife. As part of Adrienne's family, Lafayette came to have a certain affection for his destined bride which deepened later in life. As for Adrienne, a plain and severe-faced little girl, the man she was to marry became, and forever remained, her world, her reason for existence.

The wedding took place in the de Noailles' Paris mansion, with the marriage ceremony held in the mansion's chapel. The feast that followed was served on marble tables, ornate with Chinese and Japanese vases filled with flowers. So many guests had been invited that two sittings were required. Each must have gone on for hours. The finely printed, two-page menu included, among many side dishes, hors d'oeuvres and sweets—lamb, pigeon, veal, turkey, pork, chicken, eggs, ortolans, trout, eels and oysters. By the hour the last surfeited guest had departed and the teenaged couple retired to their newly decorated crimson and gold bedroom, candles were sputtering low in the chandeliers.

As an old man, Lafayette recalled this betrothal in an interview with Jared Sparks, a post-revolutionary American journalist, historian, minister, professor and president of Harvard University. At the time of the interview, Sparks was publishing a magazine called the *North American Review.* The two men—Sparks in his mid-thirties, Lafayette almost twice that age—were conversing in the publisher's office.

"Marriages made in Paris," he told Sparks, "are contrary to nature, one might almost say to justice . . . I much prefer your American custom, the young making their free choice of partners. . . . My own betrothal was a very foolish way to making a match, although in this instance, it turned out happily."

A year after the conventional marriage came conventional housekeeping. The young marquis and marquise were established in Paris, the setting considered correct for young marrieds at their social level. With the death of Louis XV and the accession of Louis XVI to the throne, the de Noailles, who were close to the new monarch, built themselves another mansion not far from the king's palace at Versailles. Lafayette and Adrienne were presented at court and Lafayette commissioned as a captain in the Noailles Dragoons, soldiers picked by the family from the Black Musketeers. The king had appointed Adrienne's father commander of that regiment. Court life, military life, the life expected by a couple who had obediently united two of the foremost families of France; this was the life the couple obediently led.

Now and then, Lafayette left Adrienne to spend intervals at Chavaniac, where he had affairs to oversee. He was building two schools for the children of villagers and he had enticed a doctor to take up residence there. He was also negotiating with provincial authorities for the right to hold a weekly market in the village and two annual fairs. These, he rightly believed, would bring more income to the farmers, which would in turn help support the schools and the doctor. To make Chavaniac accessible to patrons, he built a road into the village over which families and produce could be carted. His petition for this commerce was well received and he, himself, opened the first fair, surrounded by stalls filled with round wheels of cheese, sheaves of grain, strings of plump sausages, sides of bacon, pink hams, fragrant fruits, fresh vegetables, and livestock, grunting, baaing, neighing, squawking, mooing.

Not until he and Adrienne had been married for nine years did he suggest that she accompany him on these returns to his root land. She made no fuss. However, it was she who, when he did bring her along, pointed out what was missing in the Chavaniac development. All that grain—and no mill. With his blessing she established one.

None of the Chavaniac intervals were as long as Lafayette would have liked, nor were they as frequent. In the early years of his marriage, the de Noailles web held him in the society of nobility. Not as docile as Adrienne, he made no secret of his contempt for court routine. Appointed to the household of the Count of Provence, the king's brother, he found himself expected to hold the count's shirt and slippers at the *levée,* the daily robing ceremony of royalty. He managed to get out of this, to him, dubious honor by insulting the count. At a gathering where his lordship was showing off his excellent memory, Lafayette remarked that everyone knew memory served fools as a substitute for brains. He was expelled from the household.

At the same time, Lafayette admired in his brother-in-law, Paul, the young Viscount de Noailles, all the social gifts he himself lacked. The viscount had style. Women lost their heads and their hearts over him. A skilled horseman, successful stag hunter and a rousing good drinker, he was also a man's man. Once, when Lafayette was so drunk his friends had to pile him into a carriage, he kept insisting, "Don't forget to tell the Viscount de Noailles how much I drank."

Lafayette's admiration for Paul provokes a question. Did he genuinely detest the manner of life in which Paul excelled, or was his disdain for the court a pretense, a cloak for chagrin at being unable to compete? Never mind. Whether real or pretended, his disgust could make him physically sick. At one court party, he heard a story about a prominent actress, a certain Mademoiselle Arnould and her two lovers, the Prince d'Henin who paid for her favors and her hairdresser, whom she paid. With both men present in her dressing room one morning, the actress was supposed to have asked: "Well, whose turn is it today?" Lafayette excused himself from the party with his handkerchief to his mouth.

By such reactions, Lafayette earned the reputation of a prude. And nothing could be a more amusing game for scandalmongers than to reduce a prude to standard court level, to show that he was not, after all, beyond the reproach with which he seemed to regard others.

So a mistress was dreamed up for Lafayette. She was Aglä̈e de Puget de Barbantane, lady-in-waiting to the Duchess of Chartres, and wife of Count Phillippe Antoine de Hunolstein, member of the household of the Duke of Chartres. She was also the duke's mistress. The gossip linking her with Lafayette was set in motion by Louis Pettit de Bachaumont, author of *Mémoires Secrets,* a bestseller on the sex life of the court.

De Bachaumont was never strong on evidence and the evidence to support this particular story is particularly weak. He based it on an unsigned letter in which the writer agrees to renounce his relationship with Aglä̈e at the request of her mother who fears for her daughter's reputation. The handwriting in the letter has the cramped, angular appearance of

Lafayette's. And the date line is Chavaniac. End of de Bach-aumont's evidence.

That de Bachaumont possessed such a document there is no doubt. The question is who wrote it? The letter is laden with mistakes in grammar and spelling. Lafayette's written English was frequently faulty, but his French—never. Fur-thermore, the fiery, swashbuckling Duke of Chartres would have been most unlikely to share Agläe, or for that matter, any of the stable of favorites whom he was accustomed to transport on weekends to his country estate.

Even had the Duke not been as possessive of this troupe as he was, it seems unlikely that Lafayette, who retched at the capers of Mademoiselle Arnould could be attracted by any member of the Duke's weekend orgies. The truth—of no in-terest to gossip peddlers—may well have been that Lafayette was, by temperament, asexual. His letters and memoirs show no interest in women as sexual creatures. On the contrary, as he once wrote to the Viscount de Noailles: "I do not like girls . . . but so long as they can keep my amiable friends happy as lovers, their good taste will reconcile me." He ac-cepted them as a fact of life, but—beyond producing children to carry on the family heritage—not as a fact of his life.

In the opinion of one of Lafayette's close friends, Louis Philippe, Count de Ségur, whose memoirs give many intimate views of Lafayette, the letter of Agläe was a forgery invented as a court joke. Certainly linking the name of the shy, awk-ward Lafayette with one of the court's most flagrant cour-tesans was the type of tidbit which would have provoked the same scathing laughter as Lafayette's ballroom bumbling. Equally amusing could be the pretended concern of Agläe's mother for her daughter's reputation!

The amusement continued for several years—with varia-tions. One of these was that Lafayette tried to persuade Agläe to become his mistress, but she would have none of him. Possibly this rumor might have come nearer to the truth, for it was as fashionable for young men about Paris to have mistresses as it was for them to down quantities of wine. Once again, as when Lafayette had hoped that Paul de Noailles would be impressed with his drunkenness, he might have been trying to ape a fashion for which he lacked the temperament, secure in the knowledge that any favorite of the Duke of Chartres lay beyond his reach. However, when a song popular at intimate social gatherings linked his name with Agläe's, he was revolted. "I am the victim of a malicious imagination," he declared.

Was Lafayette's disinterest in women the result of his lack of attraction for them? In later life, when he rose to fame, they became his fans, but in youth he certainly didn't cut a come-hither figure. Or was his attitude the outcome of childhood years dominated by a totally female household? Whatever the reason, the lack of sex interest in his life left room for one grand passion to clutch him wholly: the passion for human rights.

With the young aristocrats of his time, the idea of rights unrelated to social rank, was more of a fashion than a passion, and in the beginning Lafayette's interest was mere youthful romanticism. The Count de Ségur recorded: "We found pleasure in descending as long as we believed we could climb up again when we wished . . . we tasted at the same time the advantages of the patrician and the delights of plebian philosophy."

Lafayette and his circle of comrades met regularly at the Café of the Wooden Sword in the Montmartre section of Paris, to exchange views on a high-minded reorganization of society—with frequent toasts to the Common Man in fine Beaune wine. The young enthusiasts put on a play at court which was a satire on the arrogance of the Parlement, the French National Chamber of Justice. Lafayette starred in the role of Prosecutor General. At the Comédie-Francaise and the Opéra Comique, the principal theatres of Paris, or in smaller off-boulevard theatres like D'Ambigu-Comique, le Théatre des Associés and les Variétés Amusantes, his group and other claques of young nobles applauded wildly so-called "republican" scenes, which praised the collective wisdom of the people and decried abuses of the lower by the upper classes. To the French of Lafayette's time, the word republican meant revolutionary.

Among favorite dramatists were two philosophers, Francois-Marie Voltaire and Denis Diderot. Along with the philosopher and political theorist, Jean-Jacques Rousseau and a corps of pamphleteers and journalists, these writers belonged to a movement known as the "Enlightenment." They mercilessly battled the Establishment and the established institutions which protected the power of the privileged with scant attention to the needs of the ordinary people who were the nation's majority. And they had a great deal to do with the increase in public access to information which characterized the first three-quarters of the eighteenth century. Newspapers, once solely the organs of government, were founded by private individuals. The government organs had printed what they thought sufficient for the people to know. The private publishers exposed what they thought the people had a right to know. In addition, pamphlets on political and economic matters multiplied.

In a day when a *lettre de cachet,* an order signed by the king could legally imprison a man without a trial, without his even knowing what offense he was supposed to have committed, insistence on civil liberties was considered insistence on treason. But insist these writers did and the tide of their popularity kept rising. The monarchy had reason to fear the impact of their views. Such thinking hurried the day of revolution.

The Revolution which came in 1789 was not an uprising of the hungry poor, the physically underprivileged. At no time during that period was there a nationwide shortage of food. Paris might demonstrate over the lack of bread, but except when drought struck, the wheat fields of Normandy, Picardy, Dauphiny and upper Provence continued to ripen gold. France was fat and fertile; the shortages occurred because transportation of produce was disrupted and labor for processing it displaced. The mind, not the stomach triggered the rebellion. Citizens bombarded by publications of the Enlightenment wanted to put theories into practice. They applied the theories to their own situations and came up with provocative questions. Why should the nobility be exempt from military service? Why should the church own one-fifth of all the land in France? Why should a man be jailed because the king said so? Why should the tax burden fall most heavily on the least wealthy? Why not an open society with equality of privilege?

In this climate of surge toward political reform, Lafayette and his generation grew up. Nonreader that he was, Lafayette probably read at first hand little of the reformist literature. But his friends did, and the spirit was as infectious as it was chic. Then, in the summer of 1775, at a Black Musketeers regimental reception in Metz for the Duke of Gloucester, brother of the English king, George III, came Lafayette's opportunity to practice what was being preached. The duke, not many years Lafayette's senior, was not in sympathy with his brother's conduct of colonial affairs in America. He was one of a group of young nobles who were the English counterpart of Lafayette's Cafe of the Wooden Sword rebels. Lafayette was seated next to him. His usual boredom at such ceremonies was suddenly punctured by the duke's ardent defense of the Americans who had taken up arms against the soldiers King George had dispatched to enforce his will in the colonies. With characteristic impulsiveness, Lafayette decided then and there to join the American Revolutionary Forces. The following day he went directly to Silas Deane in the American Consulate in Paris. Deane's job there was to recruit French aid for the American cause. He willingly accepted Lafayette's offer to serve, provided the Continental Congress, the colonies' elected government agreed.

More than the liberty virus had prompted that offer. Lafayette had never forgotten that his father had been killed by English cannon. He grew up with a resentment of the English, nurtured by the women in black at Chavaniac. In his memoirs, he included the "humbling of England" along with the "good of my country and the happiness of mankind" as motives for his military and political life. Enlisting in the colonies' Continental Army also provided a further advantage: escape from a way of life which gave him little challenge or pleasure.

"I viewed the greatness and littleness of the court with contempt," he later recorded, "the frivolities of society with pity, the minute pedantry of the army with disgust, and oppression of every sort with indignation. The attraction of the American Revolution transported me suddenly to my place . . . I could, at the age of nineteen, take refuge in the alternative of conquering or perishing in the cause to which I had devoted myself."

But his decision was more quickly and easily made than carried out. When his father-in-law heard of Lafayette's intentions, he persuaded the King to assign him to a French mission in England. Lafayette was forced to accept the appointment, but his stay was brief. In much the same manner as he had gotten himself expelled from the household of the Count of Provence, he provoked his expulsion from the English court. He refused to drink to the health of King George.

When he returned to Paris he learned from Deane that the Americans were not nearly so eager to accept his aid as he was to give it. There was the matter of his transatlantic passage. Who was to bear the cost? And who was to pay his Continental Army salary? The Continental Congress had no funds to spend on foreigners. Scraping up the money to pay and equip their own men was a task already tough enough. Lafayette solved the financial problem by buying, equipping and crewing at his own expense a stout vessel which he named, *La Victoire,* in anticipation of an American victory over the English. He also volunteered his services without pay. In the meantime he had joined forces with a German-born, soldier-adventurer, Johann von Kalb, who, becoming a French citizen, had taken the name Jean de Kalb. De Kalb had also gained access to the American Army through Silas Deane. He and Lafayette planned to set out together.

Still Lafayette's difficulties were not done with. The British Ambassador in France, getting wind of Lafayette's scheme, promptly protested to the French Government, which issued a warrant for Lafayette's arrest. Tipped off, Lafayette hid out for three days in De Kalb's house and dispatched his vessel to a Spanish port, Los Pasajes. His father-in-law, furious at Lafayette's desertion of rank and family, sent soldiers hunting for him. The King issued orders that he was to join the de Noailles family in the southern French port of Marseilles and travel with them to Italy. Lafayette eluded all orders, all searchers. Disguising himself as a courier, he traveled secretly to Spain with De Kalb to join his ship—deliberately skipping a farewell to his pregnant wife. Not even she was to know his whereabouts until he reached America. On shipboard two servants and a few close associates awaited him. On a raw April Sunday of 1777, a year and eight months after he had resolved to join the Continental Army, he set sail in pursuit of his goal.

On the high seas still more obstacles arose. The ship's papers, he discovered, were made out for a stopover in the West Indies. There, where both the French and English were colonial landlords and freebooters, he was almost certain to be arrested. He ordered the captain to sail straight for the United States. The captain refused. He had eight thousand dollars worth of cargo aboard for West Indian ports. Lafayette bought the cargo from him. *La Victoire* sailed on.

Then, between bouts of seasickness, Lafayette settled down
to the task he had set for himself on the long crossing: continuing the study of the English language to which he had
been exposed in London.

On April 25, 1777, *La Victoire* finally anchored near
Charleston. Lafayette and De Kalb were met by a Major
Benjamin Huger and warmly greeted as a godsend. The purpose of their voyage took, temporarily, second place to the
festivities staged in their honor. Yet even in the gaiety Lafayette detected a vast difference between the culture of the
court he had left behind and that of the new society he was
entering. He wrote home remarking on the American "simplicity of manners . . . love of country and liberty, the de-
lightful equality that reigns everywhere." He began to feel
more at home in their ways than in French ways. "The re-
semblance in their thinking to my own . . . is striking," he
commented. For almost a fortnight the newcomers reveled
in their welcome. Then they set out for the country's capital,
Philadelphia.

Lafayette had intended to sell *La Victoire* in Charleston
and use the proceeds to procure another ship to Philadelphia. He discovered, however, that in making the trans-
action for *La Victoire* he had signed an agreement which
called for her resale in France, with the captain being paid
from the proceeds. Such had been his haste to achieve his
objective that he had barely read the documents he had
signed.

It was therefore necessary to journey by land. He raised
a few thousand dollars on his personal signature in Charleston and purchased three coaches and eight horses. On June
25th, the cavalcade headed for Philadelphia with Lafayette
and de Kalb in the lead coach, preceded by one of Lafayette's
servants riding horseback and wearing the uniform of a
French hussar. His second servant rode alongside. The procession had too much panoply and too little practicality for

the route between Charleston and Philadelphia. Most of it was a mere wilderness trail.

Four days out of Charleston the party was forced to abandon the coaches. Rocks and ruts had disjointed them. Some of the horses had died. Some of the men were racked with fever contracted in swampland. Mosquitoes and flies welted the exposed parts of their bodies. Discarding almost all of their remaining luggage—much had been stolen on overnight stops—they pushed on, partly on horseback, partly on foot.

The forlorn and bearded men who arrived in Philadelphia after thirty-two days of such travel would have been unrecognizable in Paris. Lafayette was experiencing a side of the American coin quite different from the festive exposure in Charleston. The group found lodgings and the following morning, Lafayette, making himself as presentable as he could, called at the office of the President of the Continental Congress, Henry Laurens of South Carolina. Laurens's secretary gave Lafayette a chilly reception. Come back tomorrow, he was told. He did. And the next day. And the next. He was confronted with a new hurdle: the touchy feelings of the rough and ready volunteers from farm, field and forest who in large part made up the Continental Army, and whose sentiments the Congress had to consider. These American individualists were not about to take orders from a foreign officer, especially a titled one.

Despite his equality-minded principles, Lafayette apparently never gave thought to serving without an officer's commission. He cooled his heels for four days in antechambers of the Congress before the problem was resolved by giving him a commission without command. On the 31st day of July, 1777, the Congress somewhat gingerly declared:

Whereas the Marquis de Lafayette, out of his great zeal to the cause of liberty, in which the United States are engaged,

has left his family and connexions, and at his own expense
come over to offer his services to the United States, without pension or particular allowance, and is anxious to serve
our cause:
    *Resolved* that his service be accepted and that in con-
sideration of his zeal, illustrious family and connexions, he
have the rank and commission of Major General of the
Army of the United States.

A copy of the resolution was sent to Lafayette along with
the scarf of office. Still, no specific assignment followed the
commission. He was considering going home when Benjamin
Franklin, representing the United States in Paris, wrote
George Washington, Commander of the Continental Army,
suggesting that the General take Lafayette under his wing at
headquarters in Morristown, New Jersey. Franklin empha-
sized the useful effect that this gesture might have in influential French circles from which he was seeking help for the
American cause.

Washington responded by appointing Lafayette as his aide.
In his memoirs, Lafayette recalls the circumstances at their
first meeting. He describes the men in the Commander's
camp as "ill armed, ill clothed. . . . The best dressed," he
says, "wore hunting shirts."

On greeting him, Washington said, "We must feel em-
barrassed to exhibit ourselves before an officer who has just
quitted French troops."

Lafayette replied, "It is to learn and not to teach that I
came hither."

Thus, when Washington was forty-nine and Lafayette
twenty, a twenty-two-year-long friendship between the two
men began. Washington came to regard Lafayette with the
affection of a father for his son, and Lafayette returned the
affection with admiration and respect. Later in life he hung
on the wall of his Chavaniac study, opposite his framed copy

of the Declaration of Independence, one of Gilbert Stuart's portraits of the American leader.

As Washington's aide, Lafayette dropped the title Marquis. Rank-and-file Americans, unable to pronounce his name, called him "General Feyet." He strove almost to out-American them in order to win their regard. His English, though still halting, daily became more relaxed, losing the textbook formality that marks a beginner in a foreign language. He ate hardtack instead of bread, salt pork instead of sausage. He drank hard cider instead of wine. He exchanged his plumed tricorne hat for the squat headgear worn by the Continental soldiers, his fitted epauletted waistcoat for the type of bulky greatcoat worn by Washington.

Within a year Washington requested the Congress to give him command of a division of two thousand Virginia Light Troops and Congress complied. One day, after administering to his men an oath of allegiance to "free, independent and sovereign states of the United States," Lafayette commented, "It is rather strange that the oath of renunciation of Great Britain and its king . . . should be administered by a twenty-year-old Frenchman." To him personally, the act was also doubtless gratifying. It provided outlets for expression both of his resentment against England and his growing attachment to the United States.

So began Lafayette's first experience with revolution—an experience which was to ripen his modish "delight in plebeian philosophy" into a ruling passion and to prepare him for leadership in his own country. The American revolution was to be his training school, patriots like Washington and later, Jefferson, his teachers. They transformed the Marquis of the eighteenth century into the democrat of the nineteenth.

# 2

---

# TRAINING SCHOOL
## *The American Revolution*

IN 1777 the twenty-year-old divisional commander was ready for his first field action in support of the principles to which the rest of his life would be devoted. The action took place near a small creek in southwestern Pennsylvania—Brandywine.

The Battle of Brandywine occurred during the march on Philadelphia of William Howe, top general of all the British forces in the United States. He and his troops had sailed from New York aboard a fleet commanded by his older brother, Admiral Richard Howe. They landed in Chesapeake Bay, near Elkton, Maryland. The brothers' action was in direct contradiction to orders from the British War Minister, Lord George Germaine. General Howe was supposed to be marching north, not sailing south. He had been told to proceed up the Hudson River to meet and support General John Burgoyne who was coming down from Canada via Lake Champlain.

Howe had a reason for going off on his own. His theory was that if he could capture the capital city—the British already held Boston and New York—while his brother blockaded the coastline, he could then wear the Americans down without further bloodshed. A prominent member of the Whig Party, which shared the views of the French Enlightenment and was opposed to British behavior toward America, he had promised his following in England to try to win by persuasion instead of artillery. He and his brother had already put forth their views in a meeting the preceding year with a delegation from the Continental Congress. Vainly, they had offered the Americans peace terms. Admiral Howe had spoken of their reluctance to conquer by arms.

Retorted Benjamin Franklin: "We will do our utmost to save your lordships from that embarrassment."

General Howe did capture Philadelphia, but in the meanwhile Burgoyne, left without support, was trapped at Saratoga and forced to surrender with five thousand troops to General Gates, providing the Americans with the first mass victory of the war. Howe's failure to back up Burgoyne was one in a series of British blunders by which they helped defeat themselves.

The importance of Brandywine Creek was not only that Howe must cross it to reach Philadelphia from Elkton, but also that the creek led into a stream feeding the Delaware River. To hold Philadelphia, once captured, Howe needed to control the Delaware basin. On September 11, 1777, he engaged the American general, John Sullivan, at Brandywine. Sullivan's men, outranked, outflanked and out of control were fleeing in panic when Lafayette arrived, having been dispatched to the scene by Washington. In halting English, Lafayette rallied the routed men. His division was not sufficient to turn the tide, but he was able to hold the rear guard long enough to permit an orderly retreat.

In the course of the fighting he was wounded in the right knee. He was unaware of the wound at first. All his senses were trained, with the singular intensity of which he was capable, on organized—and therefore lifesaving—retreat. Suddenly he reeled in the saddle, nearly fainting from loss of blood. He would have remained in the field, nonetheless, had it not been for Washington, who had subsequently hastened there. Washington ordered him to a nearby farm and sent two surgeons to attend him, with instructions to treat him "as my own son."

Lafayette spent the next two months immobile, under medical care, chafing. "I lie here useless to the American cause," he wrote Adrienne, "while my commander struggles to prevent the fall of Philadelphia and the taking of our fortifications on the Delaware River." Even Washington's praise for his conduct at Brandywine didn't console him. Special note had been taken of Lafayette's valor in Washington's order of the day.

By November, however, he was well enough to join one of Washington's ablest officers, General Nathanael Greene in reconnoitering British positions across the Delaware. With three hundred men he surprised and routed a contingent of four hundred Hessians near Gloucester, New Jersey. Then he rejoined Washington at Valley Forge. There he froze and starved through bitter weather, enduring the severe shortages of fuel, food, clothing and blankets which beset the eleven-thousand-man army and came close to conquering its morale.

With him was de Kalb, who had also been commissioned, and another foreign volunteer, the Prussian Baron von Steuben, who like Lafayette and de Kalb had made his American connection through Silas Deane. Together, the three men did much that winter to help Washington keep his army intact. Von Steuben, a tough taskmaster, disciplined the raw recruits into trained soldiers. "The exercises will keep their minds off their stomachs," he said. More than once he bellowed curses at their awkwardness, "loudly enough," Lafayette later recollected, "to be heard in Philadelphia." De Kalb was called upon to translate the curses into English. Von Steuben wanted to make sure they were understood. A hearty swear-out, he maintained, was essential to the shaping of a proper soldier.

Lafayette's touch was more intimate. He lived among the men as they lived, doing without meals when they did, managing on one ration a day when that was available, sharing his blanket with the sick, assisting surgeons in amputating frozen feet. He became known as "the soldier's friend." For him the only cheerful note that winter was news that his second child, a healthy daughter, Anastasie, had been born the preceding July. His first daughter, Henriette, had died in infancy.

In the middle of the Valley Forge ordeal, a new blow struck. General Thomas Conway persuaded Congress to set up a War Board, supposedly for the purpose of supervising conduct of the war. The chairman was General Horatio Gates, who had become a popular hero as a result of Saratoga. In secret, the Board's purpose was to force the resignation of Washington and replace him with Gates. Washington, getting wind of the plot, wrote Congress that it was no doubt "much easier and . . . less distressing . . . to draw remonstrances in a comfortable room by a good fireside than to occupy a cold, bleak hill and sleep under frost and snow." He was able to overcome the Cabal, as the Conway plot became known, but not before it had considerably hampered his plans.

At one point the War Board attempted to take Lafayette in tow. With the objective of separating him from Washington, the Board offered him command of an army in Albany, destined for an invasion of Canada. Lafayette was flattered, but he refused to accept without Washington's approval. When that was forthcoming, he and de Kalb saddled their horses and set out for Albany. What they found on arrival was disheartening. Only a few troops had been assembled and they were in almost as bad shape as the men they had just left in Valley Forge. They were ragged, hungry, cold and unpaid. Recognizing the impossibility of leading a successful invasion under these circumstances, he wrote Washington for advice. Conway was urging him to push ahead, he said, and he feared that his standing in both Europe and America would suffer if he refused—unless Congress offered him another comparable responsibility. Somewhat petulantly, he even threatened resignation, unless Congress acted.

Washington understood perfectly Lafayette's disappointment. He saw that youthful pride had been dashed and needed restoring. He wrote back: "I am persuaded that everyone will understand your prudence in renouncing the project, in pursuing which you would vainly have attempted physical impossibilities . . . However . . . your ardour may make you feel this disappointment, you may be assured that your character stands as fairly as it ever did and that no new enterprise is necessary to wipe off this imaginary stain."

Pacified, Lafayette spent some time in the Mohawk Valley, winning to the American cause Oneida Indians, who, in return for British rum, had been massacring American frontier families. In return for the gold French coins which Lafayette distributed, they shifted allegiance, and smoking the peace pipe with him, they gave him the name Kayewla, "fearsome horseman."

Meanwhile, in Philadelphia the Board of War had come to the same conclusion as Washington on the Canadian project. Members of Congress, already fearful that the impetuous Lafayette would be led into some rash measure, were much relieved when they learned that he had decided not to pursue the invasion. They passed a resolution commending his discretion. So, in March, 1778, Lafayette returned to Valley Forge and resumed his command of the Virginia Light Troops.

He returned at an auspicious time. His own country had just formed an alliance with his adopted country, an arrangement for which Benjamin Franklin had been astutely working with the French Minister of Foreign Affairs, the Count de Vergennes.

The treaty he obtained stated that neither signer would make peace with England without the consent of the other and that neither would lay down arms until America's independence was secure. Simultaneously the French king sent a note to the British Ambassador, recognizing the independence of the United States "by their declaration of July 4th, 1776." Admiral, Count Charles d'Estaing was dispatched to the United States with a fleet of twelve ships and a number of regiments.

As soon as Lafayette returned to Valley Forge from Albany, Washington ordered that the new alliance be celebrated by a full dress review of the army. Cannons boomed while Lafayette, a white sash tied shoulder to waist across his American uniform, marched up and down the lines of soldiers. "Long live the King of France! Long live the United States!" they shouted as he passed. Throughout the thirteen states that day, the French flag, embroidered with *fleur-de-lis,* flew side by side with the stars and stripes. The cause of the United States was now also the cause of France.

The union made all the difference in the world. Within the next two years, it encouraged other nations jealous of Britain's overseas power to join the fray. Although they didn't make alliances with the United States, Spain, Holland and Russia took arms against England. What the British had considered an impudent little colonial brushfire took on the characteristics of a raging European bonfire. The British were hard pressed.

In the United States, Sir Henry Clinton, who had replaced General William Howe, was ordered to evacuate Philadelphia. Against the about-to-arrive French strength, the forts in the Delaware Valley which were Philadelphia's protection would not be defensible. Nor would Admiral Howe's coastal blockade.

Washington, anticipating the withdrawal of Clinton, and anxious not to let him slip away, sent Lafayette with his division to reconnoiter the situation. British intelligence reported the mission to Clinton, who saw in it an opportunity to kidnap Lafayette. The French-American alliance made Lafayette especially dangerous to the British, putting him in an excellent position to whip up increasing support from his countrymen. The capture of "the boy," and the British called him that, would be quite a feather in Clinton's cap.

Though General Howe had already been recalled, he decided to postpone his actual departure in order to take part in Clinton's scheme, "just for the fun of it." His brother, the Admiral, readied a frigate to take "the boy" to England along with the recalled General. So sure were they of their plans that the general sent invitations to British sympathizers in Philadelphia for a "farewell banquet to meet Monsieur de Lafayette."

At midnight on June 15, 1778, the British General Grant was sent with a force of five thousand to attack Lafayette from the rear. Grey, another British general was to attack his right flank, while Clinton and Howe were to confront him head on. Altogether the British had eight thousand men to Lafayette's two thousand. Grey, Clinton and Howe reached their positions at dawn. Lafayette's scouts brought him word that he was nearly surrounded. "In the presence of my troops, it was necessary to smile at this news," Lafayette recorded.

It was also necessary to think quickly. General Grant had not yet reached his position at Lafayette's rear, having stopped for a hearty breakfast at a comfortable inn, the Broadaxe. Lafayette dispatched most of his men still farther to the Schuylkill River, which lay between them and Valley Forge, telling them to cross the stream at Matson's Ford. The decision was a long risk: Grant and his men were nearer the ford than Lafayette was.

To cover his men's retreat, Lafayette feinted a forward attack, allowing the heads of the column he kept with him to become momentarily visible at the fringe of a forest below a height known as Barren Hill. Grant, on the slopes of the hill, began to examine their movements. During the time he took to discover the feint, Lafayette rejoined the rest of the men at Matson's Ford. All two thousand managed to cross in the nick of time. "When the lobsters closed the net, they found it empty," Lafayette reported to Washington. "Lobsters" was the American slang term for British troops, derived from their scarlet waistcoats.

Lafayette also reported that word from his scouts led him to believe that Clinton would attempt to gain New York via Trenton and Monmouth, New Jersey. Accordingly, Washington sent Lafayette and General Charles Lee to intercept Clinton at Monmouth. With substantial forces, they engaged the British army there on June 28th. The battle was going well for the Americans when General Charles Lee, who had been a member of the Conway Cabal, suddenly ordered a retreat. Lafayette sent posthaste for Washington, who arrived in time to countermand Lee's orders and rally the troops. The Americans won the victory, but in the confusion, Clinton himself escaped.

Admiral Howe's fleet also escaped safely to New York, due to the storm-delayed arrival of d'Estaing with the French ships. Not until August did the Admiral anchor off Newport, Rhode Island. Newport was British-held. Washington's plan for wresting it from them was for d'Estaing to attack by sea and General John Sullivan, of the Brandywine rout, to attack by land. Lafayette and his division were to fight under Sullivan's command.

The plan worked well at first. D'Estaing soon had command of the Newport harbor and Narragansett Bay, while Sullivan controlled the northern end of the island on which Newport is located in Rhode Island Sound. Lafayette was sent aboard d'Estaing's flagship, the *Languedoc,* to greet the Admiral, a fellow Auvergnat, and to give further moves.

The two men embraced heartily. Like Lafayette, d'Estaing

was infected with the spirit of Liberty. He also shared La-fayette's resentment of the English, whom he had fought in India. He was delighted with the chance to fight them again. The admiral and the major general talked long and earnestly. At the end of their conversation d'Estaing said: "You, Mar-quis, will command the landing party of the French in-fantry."

Lafayette was jubilant. Sullivan, when Lafayette reported the d'Estaing decision to him, was not. Although he knew he had to accept the French landing on what he considered his military territory, he resented it. At the least, he intended to assert his authority by commanding the landing procedure himself. By what right did this foreign admiral confer the responsibility on a junior officer? Especially *this* officer. Sul-livan had never forgotten Washington's eulogy of Lafayette after Brandywine.

He was further displeased with d'Estaing's requests for drinking water, meat and fresh vegetables. The French food supplies had dwindled in the stormy passage and some of the men had scurvy, a disease caused by malnutrition, especially the lack of fresh vegetables and fruit. Sullivan's own supplies were none too ample; he was unwilling to share them. Pro-curing additional ones would be difficult; the British had four thousand men stationed on the mainland coast. Sullivan re-fused the French request.

D'Estaing's officers began complaining about lack of American cooperation. Moreover, they were, as Lafayette had never been, contemptuous of the American army's lack of form and particularly of the troops' homespun dress. "A bunch of Tartars," they called their new allies. Lafayette was caught in a cross fire. He tried to interpret American senti-ments to his countrymen and their sentiments to his Ameri-can comrades. The result was that both were critical of him; the French because they thought he sided with the Ameri-cans, the Americans because they thought he sided with the French.

In the middle of the controversy, the British fleet sailed from New York, intent on rescuing the beleaguered Newport garrison. Sighting the ships as a morning fog lifted, d'Estaing attacked. The naval battle waged through the sultry August day. Toward evening, the British, their vessels half-crippled, fled. The sky was blackening with thunderheads, but d'Estaing pursued the fugitives. He hoped to disable them totally. As night fell, the skies unleashed their gathering fury. Violent gusts whipped up giant waves. Rain deluged. Lightning ripped the darkness. Nature finished the battering d'Estaing had hoped to give the British. They barely managed to crawl into New York. But d'Estaing had not escaped the storm's lash either. The French fleet limped back to Rhode Island Sound.

The only facilities for repair there—at Newport—were still in British hands. D'Estaing advised Sullivan that he would have to try to make his way to Boston. Sullivan was outraged. To abandon the Newport project now, after so much time, trouble and money had been expended to organize it, would be disastrous, he said. D'Estaing replied that his ships would be useless in their present condition. Swallowing his pride, Sullivan sent Lafayette aboard the *Languedoc* to beg d'Estaing not to leave. Lafayette dutifully tried to persuade the Admiral to stay, but was rewarded only by further scorn from his countrymen. His failure brought down on his head the wrath of the Americans. Sullivan published an order of the day in which he stated, "Our allies have abandoned us." Lafayette refused to sign it, as divisional commanders like himself were supposed to do. Further, he demanded that the reference be stricken out of the order.

Washington agreed with him and Sullivan was forced to comply. Washington's decision was based on a letter Lafayette had written him:

Now, my dear General, I am going to hurt your generous feelings . . . Forgive me for it; it is not to the commander-

in-chief, it is my dearest friend, General Washington that I
am speaking. I want to regret with him the ungenerous
sentiments I have been forced to see in American breasts.
Could you believe that, forgetting any national obligations,
forgetting what they owed to that same fleet . . . instead
of resenting their accidents as those of allies and brothers,
the people turned mad at their departure, and, wishing them
all the evils in the world, treated them as a generous man
would be ashamed to treat the most inveterate enemies?
. . . Frenchmen of the highest honor have been placed in
most disagreeable circumstances; and yet, myself, a friend
of America, the friend of General Washington, I am upon
a more warlike footing in the American lines than when I
came near the British lines at Newport. It is an example
that I use my position. I fear for the future of our alliance.

The letter's respectful tone, its apologetic setting forth of
facts and tactful use of the question mark reveal a change
in the man who, only a year earlier, had sent Washington
from Albany a petulant plea for the preservation of his own
status. Lafayette at Newport was no longer worrying about
what was thought of *him*. He was worried about the cause in
which his two countries were joined.

Washington's reply contained a new lesson:

In a free and republican government, you cannot restrain
the voice of the multitude. Let me beseech you, therefore,
my good Sir, to afford a healing hand to the wound, that un-
intentionally has been made . . . I, your friend, have no
doubt but what you will use your utmost endeavors to restore harmony, that the honor, glory and mutual interests
of the two nations may be promoted and cemented in the
firmest manner.

The letter underscored a truth which Lafayette was to
grapple with many times in later life: representative government is by nature unwieldy.

Simultaneously with the letter to Lafayette, Washington wrote d'Estaing, thanking him profusely for his services and cooperation at Newport. He gave Lafayette the assignment of riding immediately to Boston with John Hancock, a native son of Massachusetts who was a member and former president of the Continental Congress. A riot had broken out when d'Estaing attempted to land. The Bostonians, informed of what Sullivan considered d'Estaing's desertion, had refused to permit repair of the French ships and had also refused to refurbish the French supplies. A French soldier had been killed in the rioting.

The assignment to calm the city was urgent. Lafayette and Hancock covered the hundred miles between Newport and Boston in ten hours, never dismounting from their saddles. Together they were able to restore order and see that d'Estaing got what he needed. Mission accomplished, Lafayette returned to Newport to aid Sullivan in the retreat necessitated by d'Estaing's departure. The Congress passed a resolution acknowledging with gratitude his "sacrifice of personal feelings" in negotiating the Boston affair and his "gallantry, skill and prudence" in expediting the retreat. Even Sullivan apologized to him.

However carefully the Sullivan-d'Estaing dispute might be smoothed over in the United States, Lafayette sensed that it could be harmful to America's cause in France. As a French nobleman who had spent sixteen months in the service of America, he saw himself as the person best equipped to prevent damage to the alliance—a task that would require his presence at the French court. Accordingly, he requested a leave of absence from George Washington. He had other reasons also for wanting to return to Paris. Now that his own country was officially at war with England, protocol demanded that he, as a military officer, make the gesture of offering his services to his king.

Finally, he wanted to see a daughter who had been born

after his departure, and he was uncomfortably aware of the fact that he had severely neglected his wife. The letter which he wrote her at this time was apologetic. The one desire of his life, he swore, was to see her again.

Washington, who agreed that Lafayette's presence was needed in France, sent the request to the Continental Congress and suggested that Lafayette also write to Congress President Laurens. Lafayette did and Laurens replied:

> I have the honour to present to Congress the letter in which you ask for a leave of absence. I am charged by the Chamber to offer you its thanks for the zeal which you have shown in defense of the just cause which it sustains, and the distinterested service which you have rendered to the United States of America. Their representatives in Congress have ordered that a sword will be offered to you by the American minister at the court of Versailles, as a testimony of its high esteem and of the affection which the people bear to you, and as a souvenir of the valour and military talents which you have shown on many occasions.

Congress also provided a letter for Louis XVI, commending Lafayette and tactfully adding: "Devotion to his sovereign has always directed his conduct comfortably to all his duties in America; it is thus that he had acquired the confidence of the United States, your faithful friends and allies, and the affection of their citizens."

The frigate *Alliance* was placed at Lafayette's disposal for the voyage home. That voyage was an even greater test of survivalship than his trek from Charleston to Philadelphia when he first arrived. Three times Lafayette was in peril of his life. He speculated dismally on ending up as "feed for cod." When he came on board he was suffering from food poisoning. He worsened, the fever mounting. Then, like a miracle, it subsided. But, barely had he begun to recover when violent gales arose, lashing the ship. She sprang a serious leak. All hands, the weakened Lafayette included, pitched in to repair the damage—which they managed to do in the nick of time.

More danger waited. Boston convicts and deserters from the British army, who had been impressed into the crew, plotted to take the *Alliance* into a British port. There they could collect the bounty which King George offered for the delivery of American ships. They were sure, furthermore, to collect an additional and no doubt sizeable reward for the delivery of Lafayette. One loyal American sailor got wind of the plot and came to Lafayette with it. He organized the other loyal sailors and a skirmish took place between the two groups. The mutineers were forced at swords' points into the hold, where they were chained for the rest of the voyage.

In February, 1779, having evaded both cod and conspiracy, an exhausted Lafayette arrived safely in Paris. It was the time of Carnival, the last festival before the onset of Lent. Night had fallen. Chair carriers and liveried coachmen transported masked gentry through the streets amid shouts of merriment. All society was on the way to balls, the most prestigious of which was that given by the Prince de Poix, a member of the de Noailles family.

The scene was a familiar one; nevertheless Lafayette was dazed by the sudden contrast between the earnest austerity of the army life he had left in America and the heedless gaiety of partying Paris. As though in a trance, he made his way to the de Noailles Versailles mansion where he found the Prince's ball at its madcap height. At 2:00 A.M. he appeared, unmasked. As one couple after another saw him, the dancing slowed to a standstill. The music stopped. Then, wildly, the aristocracy that had spurned him as a bumpkin burst into applause and cheers. The bumpkin had become a celebrity.

Not at that moment, but soon afterward he was to figure how to put this adulation to good use in behalf of his passion for the American cause. He was also to find that his initial reception was only a token of much more to come.

At first, however, his situation was delicate. Technically, the king could not overlook the fact that Lafayette had evaded the law in order to go to America. His service there had been illegal. The King couldn't even properly receive from him the Congressional letter of which he was the bearer, not immediately at any rate. His wrist must be tapped before he could be reinstated. He was placed under benevolent house arrest for two weeks in the home of the Duke and Duchess de Noailles.

It was a busy fortnight. He was *"visiblement caché,"* visibly secluded, as Madame du Deffand, the hostess of a salon where Enlightenment leaders gathered weekly, described his status. Supposedly he could see only relatives, but the relatives brought with them everyone anxious to listen to him, to question him. By virtue of the one impulsive act of joining the American Revolution, he became a symbol of the abstract principles of justice and freedom being popularly publicized as the gateway to Utopia. This man of action, Lafayette, became the darling of the intellectuals of Paris and all things American became the fashion.

In the theatre, play after play had as hero a thinly disguised prototype of Lafayette. One, *L'Amour François,* by the popular dramatist Rochon de Chabannes, raved about its "wise, brave" hero's sacrifice of "the charmers of the palace and the pleasures of town life," also his "recent wedding's cheers"— in order to answer the call of "purest patriotism" and "purest honor." When released from house arrest, Lafayette visited de Chabannes to thank him for the compliments, even though, unknowingly, the playwright had praised him for the sacrifice of precisely those "pleasures" from which he had been eager to escape! If the irony of the situation struck Lafayette, he did not say so.

In due course came the ceremonial presentation of the

sword commissioned by the Continental Congress. Golden-hilted, the blade bore the motto of Lafayette's ancestor who had fought with Joan of Arc: *Cur Non,* why not. Also engraved were the locations of the battles Lafayette had fought in America: Brandywine, Barren Hill, Gloucester, Monmouth, Rhode Island. On the bow of the hilt the inscription read "From the American Congress to the Marquis de Lafayette, 1779." Benjamin Franklin had his little grandson offer Lafayette the sword on a tasseled satin pillow.

The house arrest was over; the king commanded his presence. The audience was to take place during a levée, the robing ceremony that Lafayette so thoroughly detested. But he was more philosophical about such affairs now. He wrote to Benjamin Franklin in the American ministry in suburban Passy: "In our kingly country we have a foolish law called etiquette, that everyone, even sensible men, must follow." The levée had forced him to break an appointment with Franklin. "But I can assure you," his note continued, "that this senseless etiquette signifies that I am restored to royal favor and will enable me to press with the king and the king's ministers our common cause." America had motivated him.

At the levée the king chided Lafayette in the gentlest of terms. Lafayette took the reprimand with grace and presented the Congressional letter he had been instructed to deliver. The king read it, added congratulations to his rebuke and invited Lafayette to go hunting with him. With the bestowal of this final seal of approval, Lafayette's popularity knew no bounds. "The kisses of the ladies," he recorded, "are most gracious and most astounding."

Madame du Deffand, who had characterized his departure for the United States as "singular folly," now touted his "magnificent courage." And a considerable number of the young French began to imitate him. Among them were Lafayette's close friends, de Ségur and Paul de Noailles, also five other comrades: Alexandre Lameth and his brothers Charles and

Theodore, Antonin, Duke de Lauzon, and Adam-Philippe, Count de Custine. Like Lafayette, Alexandre Lameth and de Lauzon would later become leaders and targets in the struggle to establish a French Republic. The guillotine awaited Lauzon and de Custine. Alexandre Lameth would be shackled in an Austrian prison. For them as for Lafayette, the American Revolution was a beginning.

Lafayette was now in the position he had predicted to Franklin would be useful. He had resumed his command of the king's dragoons, but actually, he spent most of his time lobbying for stronger military support for the United States. "I left France a rebel and a fugitive," he told Franklin. "I returned a favorite and triumphant. I can put my position to work."

He was becoming a politician, but he had not yet acquired the cool judgment of the skilled political operator. His first scheme for supplying aid to America was far too imaginative to appeal to Vergennes. He suggested that ships be borrowed from Sweden, equipped and manned in France, then sailed to the States under the American flag. Aware that France's Finance Minister, Necker, opposed further expenditures in America, alliance or no alliance, he attempted to avoid Necker's veto in case he won Vergennes's approval by offering to contribute, himself, as much of the cost as possible. The remainder, he proposed, be considered as a loan only, from the French government.

However, his plan never got to Necker. Vergennes said no. Turned down, he came up with three more schemes equally unpalatable to Vergennes and other ministers in whose offices he relentlessly lobbied. One was a plan which he and Benjamin Franklin conceived together for an attack on Canada; another, plotted with the American naval commander John Paul Jones, was a sea attack on the west coast cities of England. The third was to stir up in Ireland a rebellion which would preoccupy the British.

For the latter he won the approval of the Ministers of Marine, Finance, State and Foreign Affairs. But the Minister of War was strongly opposed. The fruit of his labors was that he found himself suddenly ordered to Spain with his dragoons. The ministers were weary of his schemes.

He had been operating under a variety of handicaps. The d'Estaing incident still rankled in the ministers' minds. News from the States was not encouraging; war was going badly for the Americans in the South. The American representatives in Paris were bickering among themselves. Silas Deane had been replaced by John Adams, whose New England bluntness thoroughly antagonized Vergennes. Both Adams and Arthur Lee, another new American diplomat, antagonized Benjamin Franklin. Lee had schemed for the removal of Deane, of whom Franklin was fond. In a letter to George Washington, Lafayette implored, "For the love of God, prevent those vulgar internal quarrels whose recitation injures more than anything else the interest and reputation of America. There are two parties in France—Mr. Adams and Mr. Lee on one side and Dr. Franklin and his friends on the other . . . I do not call upon these gentlemen as often as I would like, for fear of creating discussions." Subsequently, Lee was recalled, Adams was admonished, and Lafayette, soon back from Spain, was free to work with Franklin alone.

They made an excellent team, the wily sage and the dedicated young lobbyist. The upshot of their efforts was French agreement to dispatch to America an army of six thousand, commanded by General Jean Baptiste de Rochambeau. Lafayette returned to America, this time officially, as the bearer of the good news to Washington.

He arrived in Boston on April 27, 1780, and immediately wrote Washington:

Here I am, my dear General, and, in the midst of the joy I feel in finding myself again one of your loving soldiers, I

take the time to tell you that I came from France on board
a frigate which the king gave me for my passage. I have
affairs of the utmost importance which I must communi-
cate to you alone . . .

In case my letter finds you anywhere this side of Philadelphia, I beg you to wait for me, and I assure you that a
great public good may be derived from it. Tomorrow we
go up to town and the day after I shall set up in my usual
way to join my beloved and respected friend and General.
Adieu, my dear General; you will easily know the hand of
your young soldier. My compliments to your family.

He didn't leave as soon as he expected. Celebrations of his
arrival detained him. By day, church bells chimed and cannons boomed. By night, bonfires blazed and fireworks illuminated the skies. A steady stream of officials climbed
aboard Lafayette's frigate to welcome his return. A fortnight
passed before he met Washington in Morristown and de-
livered his cheering message. Along with it he brought personal news: a son had been born to him the Christmas Eve
he had been at home, whom he had named Georges Washington Lafayette.

Washington promptly recommended that Congress rein-
state Lafayette to his old command of Virginia Light Troops.
A resolution was passed to that effect, along with commending Lafayette to public confidence—an addition which provoked sarcastic comment from Franklin. "I am glad to hear,"
he wrote from Paris, "that our legislators are still trying to
keep up with their constituents."

The reinstated commander clothed his soldiers in smart
uniforms he had brought from France. For each there was a
hat plumed with red and black horsehair and for the officers
there were swords. The Light Troops had to take some mock-
ery from other soldiers, still clad in what came to hand, but
such was the major general's popularity that his whim was
indulged as a token of would-be generosity. No hard feelings
were aroused.

Lafayette was in a unique position. A French commander of an American division, he was simultaneously a special envoy from France to the American commander in chief and his personal advisor on the use of French troops in the American army. In the latter capacity he was sent to confer with Rochambeau when a fleet of thirty-one vessels, commanded by Admiral Ternay landed the French Army in Newport, which the British had evacuated the preceding October.

The day, July 11th, was brilliant with sun. Through crowd-lined streets marched regiments of Soissonais, Bourbonnais, Bourgognais, Gascons and Basques and Savoyards— a cross-section some fifty-three hundred strong, of the fighting strength of the provinces of France. Past the statehouse and the brick markethouse they marched, past Trinity Church and Touro Synagogue, the band in the vanguard playing traditional French army airs: "Auprès de Ma Blonde" and "Dans les Gardes Françaises," the soldiers singing lustily.

The cream of the new generation in France, these seventeen to thirty-five year olds made a brilliant spectacle; the officers in blue and gold, the troops in red-lined, red-cuffed, white waistcoats, their gray breeches embroidered at the knees and their gators laced ankle to knee. Their hats were bicornes, except for the Basques, whose red berets were slung rakishly to the side. The Soissonais, commanded by the Duke de Noailles, plumed their bicornes with red and white feathers. They seemed to be favorites of the crowd, judging by the extra applause they received as they passed. Bringing up the rear was a regiment of daredevil volunteers, commanded by de Lauzon. At the head of each regiment a banner was carried, bearing the regimental motto: *Va de bon coeur,* go heartily; *En avant sur les canons,* forward astride the canons; *Le premier dans la place,* the first in the field.

But the spectacle that spellbound the crowd was only half the French contribution in support of the American rebellion. The fighting men would have been useless without the three million tons of equipment they brought with them. No need had been overlooked; Lafayette, who knew well the scarcity of supplies in America, had seen to that. Rochambeau's frigates, supply ships, cutters and transports, thirty-eight vessels in all, unloaded, in addition to the men, ten thousand shirts, ten thousand, three hundred and seventy-one pairs of boots, twelve hundred capes, twelve hundred and ten tents, one thousand picks, one thousand shovels, one thousand axes, another thousand billhooks and a thousand each of mess plates, cauldrons and canteens. And—for wooing the Indians—four thousand blue-and-red-striped blankets. There was also a completely equipped portable field hospital.

Before the landing, Lafayette had already conferred with Rochambeau. Much to Lafayette's surprise, the conference had proved prickly. Lafayette had presented the general with a letter from Washington. After stressing Washington's confidence in Lafayette, the letter continued, "All the information which he gives and all the propositions which he makes, I entreat you to consider as coming from me. I request that you will settle all arrangements whatsoever with him."

Rochambeau was not pleased. A Marshal of France, a fifty-five-year-old veteran of the war in which Lafayette's father had been killed, he was not prepared to take "propositions" from a twenty-two-year-old whom he considered a beginner in military affairs. The more enthusiastic Lafayette waxed as he outlined a proposal for the siege of New York, the less impressed was Rochambeau. The young man was too eager, too uncalculating of consequences. Didn't he realize that Admiral Ternay's fleet was already blockaded by the British off Narragansett?

"I shall not move unless I can count on command of the sea," he replied. He wrote Washington, explaining his position and requesting to see him directly.

Meanwhile the French Army sat in Newport—much to the pleasure of the French officers, who found Newport girls as flirtatious as any they had left behind. With de Noailles at the violin the French held weekly dances which every Newport girl aspired to attend. At these affairs de Lauzon, in particular, developed a reputation as a charmer; it was said that he changed girls as often as most men changed their shirts. If the fathers of Newport, most of whom were merchants or ship chandlers, had doubts about such conduct, they kept still. The French bought lavishly and they paid their bills in gold. As for the mothers, they were enchanted by the French manners and sparkle, a type of personality totally new to pioneering colonial Americans. Newport called its visitors "like beings descended from the moon."

Only Lafayette seemed impatient. Although he did invite his compatriots for grog, a hot rum drink, in his tent, he refused their invitations to make merry with them. "I have neither the time nor the taste for wenching," he wrote de Lauzon, "and I pray that you, my dear friend, do not, during this unfortunate delay, lose sight of the high purpose in which we are joined." He again appealed for an attack on New York in a letter to Rochambeau and Ternay. "I assure you gentlemen, in my own name, that this campaign is urgent . . . Even the reinforcements that may be sent from France next year will not be able to undo the damage caused by our present inaction."

Rochambeau replied that he had asked Washington for an appointment. "I shall await *his* orders," he added. Lafayette had the grace to realize that his impatience had offended Rochambeau. He wrote him an apologetic note. Rochambeau accepted the apology graciously. "My dear Marquis," he responded, "allow me to reply to you as a father would to . . . a son. If I pointed out to you what displeased me . . . it was only because I understood that your ardor had prevailed over the wisdom of your judgment." Washington agreed to meet Rochambeau in Hartford, and the two men sent an envoy to France with a joint request for more money, troops and ships.

The need was urgent—the war was not going well for the Americans. The British controlled the seas; Clinton held New York. In a battle at Camden, South Carolina, de Kalb and nine hundred others of the Continental Army had been killed; the British General Charles Cornwallis now controlled much of the South.

On top of these tragedies came the treason of Benedict Arnold. General Arnold was in command of the Hudson River fortress at West Point. A hero in earlier battles, he had not advanced in rank as rapidly as he thought he should. Resentful, and egged on by his wife who was a Tory sympathizer, he opened negotiations with Clinton to hand the post over to the British. The go-between was the British spy, Major John André. André, with the plans of the fort in his boots, was caught by three American militiamen. He was brought to Washington's headquarters at Tappan, New York, for court-martial.

Lafayette was one of the judges. The verdict was unanimous: death. Lafayette had voted as he knew he must—as his adopted compatriots expected that he would. But after the trial he walked, weeping, from the courtroom. He went straight to Washington's lodgings. André, he pleaded, had only been carrying out an assigned duty. He begged for pardon, or at least that André be shot as a soldier, rather than hung as a criminal.

There was no way Washington could grant such a request. A few years earlier, the British had hanged as a spy Nathan Hale, a young militia officer assigned by Washington to get information about British forces on Long Island. Hale had also been doing no more than his duty, Washington reminded Lafayette, and he had not even been given the courtesy of a court-martial. The hanging of André would even a score that rankled among the American troops. Lafayette understood, but he refused to attend the hanging. He remained in his quarters. Washington also remained in his.

Arnold escaped to a British warship in the Hudson and was made a brigadier general in Clinton's army. Clinton sent him to command the British garrison at Hampton Roads, Virginia, from which point he launched a series of raids on Richmond. Washington decided to dispatch Lafayette to the troubled territory. His instructions were to capture Arnold, if possible, and "execute the punishment due to his treason and desertion in a most summary way." Washington counted on this assignment to transform Lafayette's brooding over the André hanging, and his own part in it, into the purposeful action which was Lafayette's strength. Washington was right. Lafayette looked on the mission as an opportunity to revenge André's death.

But there was more to the mission than the chasing down of Arnold. Occupied with northern campaigns, Washington had been able to send little aid to the beleagured governor of Virginia. Von Steuben was in Virginia, in charge of the few regulars stationed there. His blunt demands for support from local civil and militia officers had stirred statewide shocks of ruffled feelings. The second half of Lafayette's task was to repair these feelings and in effect to take over from the crusty Prussian, without wounding his pride. He must also avoid offending the overall commander in the south, General Greene. A delicate business, this, especially for the headstrong Lafayette. Yet Washington's judgment in thrusting him into it was to be more than justified. The Virginia campaign, culminating in the British surrender at Yorktown, proved to be Lafayette's greatest contribution to American victory.

# 3

## *Their Man in France*

THE Virginia assignment was so ticklish that Lafayette approached it with unwonted caution. The slowness of pace gave him time to understand other men's problems, to develop feeling for them. He found the independent spirit of the sturdy Virginians appealing—they reminded him of his fellow Auvergnats. He could identify with the tobacco farmer who steadfastly refused to lend his horses to the army: how would the man plow his fields? And he was filled with admiration for the keen intellect of Virginia's hard pressed governor, the personage who would become his chief political preceptor for most of the next half-century.

The governor was Thomas Jefferson, the author of the American Declaration of Independence. In letters from March 8 to March 16, 1781, Jefferson broke Lafayette in on the sort of difficulties that must be continuously faced in defending the state. On March 8th, he wrote:

> The Quartermasters are exerting themselves to get horses. Their exertions are slow and doubtful. Oxen, I apprehend, must be used in some measure for the artillery . . . Scows, I am afraid cannot be used for the transportation of your

cannon on the wide waters where your operations will be carried on. We shall endeavor to procure other vessels as best we can. The total destruction of our trade by the enemy has put it out of our power to make any great collection of boats. Some armed vessels of public and some of private property are held in readiness to cooperate . . . but they cannot venture down until command of the water is taken from the enemy . . . I shall continue to exert my best endeavors to have in readiness what yet remains to be done, and shall with great pleasure meet your desires on this important business, and see that they be complied with as far as our condition will render practicable.

On March 12th:

I fear the number of boats requisite for your men and cannon will be very defective. Baron Steuben thinks twenty necessary, but there cannot be half that number procured. . . . I think it proper, therefore, to reduce your expectations from which should be ready to what probably will be ready, and even calculating on probabilities, I find it necessary to reduce my expectations from time to time. I know that you will be satisfied to make the most of an unprepared people who have the war now for the first time seriously fixed in their country and have, therefore, all those habits to acquire which their northern brethren had in the year 1776.

On March 14th:

I must beg the favor of you . . . to give me very timely notice when anything like want shall be approaching, because time is requisite in this state to comply with any call.

To these communications, Lafayette replied:

Your Excellency's favors . . . having come yesterday to hand, I beg leave most respectfully to offer my thanks . . .

From an early period, Sir . . . have I been used to those inconveniences that are . . . compensated by the number-less blessings of a popular government. Whenever personal labors or more difficult ways may conduct to . . . public good, duty as a Servant of the Public and affection as a Lover of America shall ever prompt me to adopt every measure that you may think more suitable to the temper of the people, or the state of our circumstances—the in-terest being commun [*sic*] to all engaged in this cause.

My stay in this place have [*sic*] not yet permitted me to be thoroughly acquainted with the local situation before I can either take command of the troops or make more particular applications for our wants—But I hope that . . . before I leave this place I may be able to write a more minuted let-ter to your Excellency.

What a contrast between this reply and the letter Lafayette had sent Rochambeau and Ternay only eight months earlier: *"I assure you gentlemen, in my own name, that this campaign is urgent."*

Relating to the community was not Lafayette's only prob-lem in Virginia, however. On top of the unreadiness of the local population and local militia, was piled the discontent of the regular troops. Ill-fed and ill-clothed, unaccustomed to the southern climate and suffering from fevers and malnu-trition, they were deserting daily. Lafayette determined to exercise as little as possible his right to impress, that is to demand supplies from the countryside. He obtained proper provisions from merchants in Baltimore on his personal credit. He persuaded the women of Baltimore to make the soldiers' clothing. Then, after frankly outlining dangers ahead, he offered freedom to go home to any soldier unwill-ing to follow him. Not a man accepted. There were no more desertions.

A month later, Lafayette was forced to impress. He re-ceived intelligence that Clinton was sending troops south under the command of General Phillips for an attack on Virginia, while Cornwallis moved north. The attack was to be centered on Richmond. The information led him, as he wrote Jefferson, to conclude that he must advance from Head of Elk, Maryland, where he was stationed, to Richmond:

> . . . by rapid and forced marchs [*sic*] . . . and, to impress a great number of wagons and horses to forward our movement. This measure I have reluctantly adopted, but as uncommon dangers require uncommon remedies, thought that the State of Virginia being so far interested in this movement, they would put up with momentary inconveniences provided we could more rapidly advance to their succor.

Lafayette had withdrawn to Head of Elk from the Williamsburg area after a defeat of the French fleet by the British at the head of Chesapeake Bay. The original plan had been for him to proceed to Hampton Roads by land, while the fleet sailed in by sea. The land and sea forces together were to effect the capture of Benedict Arnold. The plan had been hampered by the French defeat, as well as by the impossibility of combining without impressment, the men, provisions, ammunition, and transportation required for the maneuver. Whenever Lafayette obtained one of these necessities, he found that at least one of the others—and sometimes all three—were lacking. Consequently the capture of Arnold had been abandoned, much to Lafayette's chagrin. Some months later Arnold escaped to Canada.

Now, however, Phillips's descent from the north plus Cornwallis's ascent from the south with the objective of closing in on Richmond left him no choice but to get to Richmond before they did. He received Jefferson's full support for the impressment required. The Virginians, having warmed to the restraint shown by the French commander, also did their level best to get him to Richmond ahead of Phillips, who was expected to arrive before Cornwallis. Lafayette entered the city on April 29, barely in time. Phillips had reached Manchester on the bank of the James River across from Richmond the night before.

A month later Jefferson was able to win, from the Virginia Legislature, broad powers for Lafayette to impress men and material, with the exception of "stud horses and brood mares, because to take them would be to rip up the hen which laid the golden eggs." Lafayette shared these supplies liberally with von Steuben, a move which averted any need for the demanding general to confront reluctant farmers, and thus prevented any further ruffling of local feelings. It also gave von Steuben the wherewithal to proceed in his customary one-two-three fashion and dissolved any huff with which he might have greeted Lafayette's assignment to Virginia. When he got what he wanted, von Steuben was not a man to bother with such trifling formalities as personal position. As for Greene, with whom Lafayette also shared supplies, he had from the beginning welcomed the skill with which he saw Lafayette devoting himself to creating unity in the defense of the Virginia sector of the south.

In Richmond, Lafayette met for the first time the statesman whose Declaration would later hang on his study wall at Chauvaniac. The two men dined only briefly together—Jefferson was about to leave for Charlottesville for a session of the state legislature. Nevertheless, their conversation then —and later at Lafayette's camp at Wilton, eight miles south of the city—was concerned with more than military problems. It progressed to a plumbing of each other's social theories.

The two men discovered that they shared common faith in what Jefferson called "the plain people," common belief that power should be delegated only by them and only to leaders they select, as against the aristocratic doctrine that government is above the people.

The tall, rangy governor, in his rumpled, careless clothing, his shirt stained at the ruffle and raveled at the cuffs, his pumps run over at the heels, cut a figure in sharp contrast to the neatly tailored officer who kept his boots polished and his hair tied back. Jefferson's unruly shock of already white hair stuck out over his ears like awning fringe; his jaw was square and uncompromising. Yet his straight-set mouth uttered in a quiet drawl the same ideas that Lafayette, pursing his delicately arched lips around the English words, enthusiastically articulated.

Statesman and soldier entertained an equal horror of the few taking advantage of the many, and an equally strong conviction on every citizen's right to express his opinion and the healthy effect on nations of the widest possible distribution of information. Jefferson, who both spoke and understood French, had read much of the Enlightenment literature. He was, in later years, as a supporter in the United States of the French Revolution, to be labeled by political enemies as an "American Voltaire who would make our sons the disciples of civil disobedience." For Lafayette, Jeffersonian philosophy became a yardstick against which to measure all political reasoning—his own and others.

The concept of "Man as a rational animal, endowed by nature with rights and with an innate sense of justice," who could "be restrained from wrong and protected in right by moderate powers confided to persons of his own choice"—the keystone of Jefferson's theory of government—became Lafayette's guiding light. The extent to which an achievement was based on this concept became his measure of its worth. Jefferson's "eternal hostility against every form of tyranny over the mind of man" was the attitude which colored Lafayette's decisions. His two interviews with Jefferson in 1781 gave a strenuous push to his development from a dabbler in the dream of an open society to an activist determined to make it come true.

Shortly after these interviews he left Richmond to pursue Phillips, forcing him to retreat from the northern bank of the James. Phillips caught a fever and died during the retreat, leaving the command to Benedict Arnold, and ordering him to connect with Cornwallis at Petersburg. In vain did Lafayette attempt to head off the meeting. The union brought together seven thousand well-equipped British troops. Against them Lafayette commanded half that many. Cornwallis took Richmond and sent a contingent to capture the legislature at Charleston. Most of the legislators, with Jefferson, escaped only a few minutes before the British entered the city.

Cornwallis was now determined to capture "the boy." He wrote to the British War Minister that this time he would not be permitted to escape. Lafayette recognized his own danger. He wrote to one of the de Noailles family that he was "devilishly busy getting himself licked." He retreated rapidly across the Rapidan and Rappahannock Rivers, where he was joined by Anthony Wayne, who had been a comrade-in-arms at Brandywine and had since won much acclaim for his daring and his successes. Thus reinforced, he decided to attack Cornwallis, who had camped on what appeared to be the only road to Albemarle Courthouse, the site of considerable Continental supplies. There he meant to cut Lafayette off from the supplies, but Lafayette turned the tables on Cornwallis. During the night he cleared an old, unused road to the storehouse and got between it and the general.

He entrenched himself so firmly that Cornwallis was afraid to attack him. Actually, even with Wayne's reinforcements, Lafayette's strength was still only two-thirds that of the British. Cornwallis could have defeated him then and there, but he was taken in by a ruse which Lafayette invented. He sent a black soldier to the British camp, pretending to be a counterspy. The soldier gave such a highly exaggerated account of the American numbers and resources that Cornwallis decided to return to Richmond.

At Richmond he received orders from Clinton in New York, who feared an attack on the city by Washington. Cornwallis was to send a detachment of troops. With this end in mind, Cornwallis withdrew to the James River, sending across most of his stores and some of his troops. He held the remaining men in close formation, believing, correctly, that Lafayette would try to attack his rear guard. He also sent out a few skirmishers, instructed to retreat as Lafayette advanced, thus leading him to the main body of the army. The trick worked; Lafayette mistook the skirmishers for the rear guard and put Wayne in charge of leading an advance against them. Wayne, of course, soon found himself face to face with massed troops. With his usual daring, he would have attacked anyway, but was prevented by Lafayette's cool order to retreat. With night coming on, a crushing defeat was avoided. Before dawn Lafayette had slipped out of his dangerous situation. Much depended upon this exercise of judgment. A defeat at that time would probably have thrown the Virginia campaign to the British.

Cornwallis, meanwhile, in accordance with Clinton's orders, took up a position at Yorktown, thus inviting ultimate defeat for the British. General Greene drove them from Charleston and left Wayne in command there. Lafayette hastened after Cornwallis and established his forces at Malvern Hill, about twenty miles from Yorktown. From this vantage point he could check British movements and prevent Cornwallis from escaping into the Carolinas.

George Washington was on his way down from New York, at which he had made a feint to keep Clinton unaware of his intention to march south. With him was a French army commanded by Rochambeau. The French Admiral, Francois-Joseph, Count de Grasse, was on his way to meet the land forces with a fleet at the mouth of Chesapeake Bay. Aboard were more French soldiers, commanded by Claude-Henri, Count de Saint-Simon. British Admiral Graves reached the Chesapeake on September 5th, with the intention of rescuing Cornwallis, but de Grasse had beaten him to the position. Graves turned away. Cornwallis would soon have against his seven thousand a combined French-American force of sixteen thousand. His doom was certain.

Saint-Simon gave to Lafayette the command of his French troops. On September 14th, they were joined by the troops of Washington and Rochambeau. The siege of Yorktown began. From the sea, de Grasse blasted the town with shot and shell. On land, French and Americans trained their siege guns on the British lines. Under cover of the joint bombardment, the allies moved closer and closer to their targets. These were two hilltop strongholds from which the British continued to sweep their opponents with a steady fire.

Eleven o'clock on the night of October 14th was set as the time the strongholds were to be stormed. A French officer, the Baron de Viomenil, commanded the attacking group for one; Lafayette led the other. Scaling the walls, Lafayette's four hundred men fought hand-to-hand. The battle was brief, ten minutes and the stronghold surrendered. Only a few minutes later came a cry from the Viomenil force, "Vive le roi!" The second stronghold had fallen.

Lafayette was particularly pleased with the showing made by his troops. In a letter to a Bostonian preacher, Samuel Cooper, he said:

> Never have my feelings been so delightfully gratified as they were on the 14th in the evening, when the American light infantry, in the sight of the armies of France . . . and England . . . stormed a redoubt, sword in hand, and proved themselves equal in this business to the grenadiers of the best troops in Europe. I long ago knew dependence was to be put on them . . . but to *see* this little affair transacted under the eyes of foreign armies gave me unspeakable satisfaction.

Five days later, on October 19, 1781, the British formally surrendered. Lafayette's leadership in the Virginia campaign which was the prelude for this final victory was praised by the Continental Congress in a resolution underscoring his "judgment and vigilance"—an observation the legislators could not have honestly made of him in the earlier days of the Revolution.

The American experience had tempered Lafayette's hotheadedness and taught him how to do much with little. But it had done more than that; it had acted out the theories stylish in the salons of Paris and shown that they were workable in practice. Man *could* have a decisive voice in his own destiny, he *would* fight and die for that right if necessary, and he *was* capable of the self-discipline self-government demanded. The Lafayette who returned to France after the American Revolution was no longer playing with ideas. He was dedicated to one idea: accomplishing in his own country the transformation he had helped bring about in the United States.

"The happiness of America is intimately connected with the happiness of the world," he observed in a letter from France to his friend Jefferson. He was convinced that in the contest between "rights and privileges" which swept the western world in his day, only those governments based on the principle of "upright . . . American liberty" could prevail. He called America "the country of my heart." He had found his grand passion.

His American friends cautioned him not to let this passion run away with his new-found judgment. Saying farewell to Lafayette and the French troops, Samuel Cooper warned:

> Do not let your hopes be inflamed by our triumphs on this virgin soil. You will carry our sentiments with you, but if you try to plant them in a country that has been corrupt for centuries, you will encounter obstacles more formidable than ours. Our liberty has been won by blood. You will have to shed it in torrents before liberty can take root in the old world.

Jefferson, too, constantly admonished Lafayette not to hope for a rapid or complete transplant of representative government into the rigid structure of French political life. It would require "time and the advance of time" to prepare people for it. Lafayette stored this advice in the back of his mind. He would later put it to sound use. He trained his first attention in France on rallying economic aid for the infant United States.

He reached the de Noailles home on January 18, 1782. Adrienne was not there. She was attending a palace party, celebrating the birth of a long-awaited son to the king and queen. News of Lafayette's arrival was brought to the gathering. Adrienne agonized. The rules of the court prevented her from leaving the party before the queen did. Marie Antoinette, not incapable of sentiment, observed her emotion. "I shall take you home immediately, my dear," she said to Adrienne, and ordered her carriage.

A large crowd had gathered outside the de Noailles house. As the queen's carriage drew up, Lafayette came out to meet it. Adrienne stepped down and swayed, half-fainting. Lafayette caught her in his arms, bowed deeply to the queen and carried his wife inside while the crowd cheered.

Seven months later a daughter was born of this reunion. Lafayette wrote of the event to Benjamin Franklin:

> Every child of mine that comes to light is a small addition to the number of American Citizens. I have the pleasure to inform you that though she was but seven months advanced, Mde. [*sic*] de Lafayette has this morning become mother of a daughter who, however delicate, in its [*sic*] beginning, enjoys a perfect health, and I hope will soon grow equal to the heartiest children.
>
> This reminds me of our noble Revolution, into which we were forced sooner that it ought to have begun—but our strength came on very fast . . . They asked me what name our daughter is to have. I want to present her as an offering

to my western Country—and as there is a good Sainte by the name of Virginie,* I was thinking it was not presuming too much to let her bear a name similar to that of one of the United States.

Franklin replied the same day he received the letter.

In naming your children, I think you do well to begin with the most ancient State. And as we cannot have too many of so good a race, I hope you and Mme. Lafayette will go thru the Thirteen. But as that may be in the common way too severe a task for her delicate frame, and children of seven months may become as strong as those of nine, I consent to the abridgement of two months for each; and I wish her to spend the twenty-six months so gained, in perfect ease, health and pleasure.

Virginie's older sister, Anastasie, maintained later that for several months after her father's return, her mother felt ill whenever her father so much as left the room. If Anastasie was right—and her credibility may be doubtful, she was only five years old at the time—Adrienne must have been often ill, for Lafayette spent precious little time even in the same house with her. He was too busy. As the Americans' man in France, he was constantly on the go, using his popularity to their advantage.

His popularity was even greater than it had been on his first return, three years earlier. One night, while attending a performance of the Opera *Iphigenia in Aulis,* he was crowned with a laurel wreath. When the chorus began to sing about an ancient Greek hero, "Achilles is crowned by the hands of Victory," the opera's star, one Mademoiselle Torquay, went

* Lafayette didn't mention that the child's full name, though she was never called by it, was Marie Antoinette Virginie. A strange combination—the name of the autocratic French Queen and the American state where British autocracy went down to defeat.

Lafayette as a teenager. *Courtesy of the Lafayette Memorial Foundation.*

Adrienne, Marquise de Lafayette. *Courtesy of the Lafayette Memorial Foundation.*

Chavaniac. *Courtesy of the Lafayette Memorial Foundation.*

The kitchen at Chavaniac. *Courtesy of the Lafayette Memorial Foundation.*

Salon, or living room, at Chavaniac. *Courtesy of the Lafayette Memorial Foundation.*

Gilbert DU MOTIER
MARQUIS DE
LA FAYETTE

Lafayette's certificate of embarcation on board *La Victoire*.
*Courtesy of the French Embassy Press and Information Division.*

Lafayette meeting with Benjamin Franklin. *Courtesy of the
French Embassy Press and Information Division.*

Washington and Lafayette at Valley Forge. *Courtesy of
the New York Public Library.*

Lafayette wounded at the Battle of Brandywine. *Courtesy of the New York Public Library.*

Lafayette with George Washington during his third trip to
the United States. *Courtesy of the French Embassy Press
and Information Division.*

to Lafayette's box to place the crown on *his* head. The audience stood to applaud, cheering. Not for a quarter of an hour could the performance be resumed.

The king made him a Maréchal-de-Camp, the equivalent of a major general, skipping over ranks to do so. The marshals of France invited him to dine with them. Not only did Lafayette have this bank account of personal esteem to draw on in lobbying for the United States; this time he had also the esteem in which the United States was held after the defeat of Cornwallis. And he had as American Ambassador and ally his good friend and wise strategist, Thomas Jefferson.

The first job they tackled was to stop imports of American tobacco from coming via England. French imports of tobacco were supervised by a group known as the Farmers-general, which had sole and complete control of the business. This monopoly was buying large quantities of Virginia and Maryland tobacco from England. Jefferson and Lafayette set out to arrange for direct import from these states.

The Farmers-general were stolidly opposed to such a move, probably because they were receiving a bribe from the British for importing through them. There was no sense trying to buck their monopoly head-on; it was too powerful. So, at Jefferson's suggestion, Lafayette persuaded the French Finance Minister, Charles de Calonne, to establish a Committee of Commerce, on which representatives of the Farmers-general, general inspectors of commerce, members of the finance minister's council and several distinguished individuals would serve. The avowed reason for setting up the Committee was to study the future of commercial relations between France and the United States. The real reason, of course, was to try to undermine the control of the Farmers-general.

Lafayette, who knew nothing whatsoever about trade relations, was also appointed to the committee. He received detailed briefings from Jefferson, which cloaked his ignorance.

"I am considered as one who has a very strange idea," he told Jefferson in reporting on the meetings, "and I don't think I can gain anything now except the hatred of the financeeing [*sic*] people, but as M. de Malesherbes was telling me in his botanic style, I am sowing seeds which will bear fruit in time. . . . The last meeting I was engaged in a hot skirmish with three very able representatives of the Farm . . . I have acquired at last a pretty compleat [*sic*] knowledge of the subject."

Actually, less time was required to bring the committee round to his "very strange idea" than Malesherbes, President of the Paris Court of Aids, predicted. Under the persuasion of the Committee, the Farmers-general decided it would be a patriotic gesture (no doubt worthy of royal recompense) to renounce their contract with London merchants and grant it to Americans. But there was a rub in the decision. They granted the contract to just *one* American, the financier Robert Morris. To him went the exclusive privilege of serving them in America. The Jefferson-Lafayette goal had not been solely to obtain trade for America. They also wanted to get rid of the unnecessary middlemen who made their profits at the expense of both American producers and French consumers. All they had succeeded in doing so far was to exchange British middlemen for an American.

They went to work on the next step. Jefferson was able to get the United States to postpone for six months the date when Morris's lease would begin. During that time, Lafayette induced the finance minister's council to force the Farmers-general also to purchase "from such other merchants as shall offer fifteen thousand hogsheads of tobacco at thirty-four, thirty-six, and thirty-eight livres the hundred, according to the quality." The result saved from twelve to sixteen livres the hundred that had formerly made up the middlemen's commission, and which could now be divided between the grower and the customer.

In similar fashion Lafayette and Jefferson worked together to nourish commerce between France and the New England states—especially to obtain tax-free entrance into France of whale oil. To attain their end they stressed that America would sooner and better be able to repay her war debt to France if France would buy American products. The argument was timely because the French treasury was in precarious shape. Jefferson sent Lafayette a working paper consisting of a list of twenty-two American commodities available for export in quantities ranging from sixty thousand barrels of turpentine to six hundred and sixty thousand barrels of flour. It included whale oil, fish and fish bones, livestock, Indian corn, timber, hops and thirteen other agricultural products or raw materials.

Along with the export list was a catalog of American imports—seventy-two of them. An accompanying memo suggested that France check on the import list those items she could supply.

Through this approach, Lafayette and Jefferson hoped to build up for the United States a commercial credit of about two hundred seventy-five thousand louis—enough to pay off gradually the debt America owed France. Again using the Committee of Commerce as his sounding board and pressure instrument, Lafayette went to work on the assignment. In a few months he achieved remarkable results. America was given three tax-free French ports into which to bring her merchandise. The tariff in all ports on brandy was abolished. Tariff was also abolished for one year on whale oil, potash, furs, leather and timber. A tax on French ships built in America was cancelled. So too was a prohibition on exporting French firearms to the United States.

In the middle of this campaign for trade concessions, Lafayette visited the States. His mission, as an unofficial ambassador of goodwill approved by his government was to update the Continental Congress and particularly the local legislatures and the citizenry on progress in the negotiations. He traveled to every state except the Carolinas and Georgia. He made speeches in New York, Albany, Hartford, Worcester, Boston, Philadelphia, Baltimore, Richmond, Alexandria, and throughout Pennsylvania. Ceremonies were held at all the battlefields on which he had fought.

The only let-up in the five month schedule was eleven days of rest with Washington, in his home, Mount Vernon. There the two men passed the time in conversation on issues close to their hearts. They discussed the future of America and the present urgent need to unite the loosely knit confederation of states into a federation with a strong central government. They projected what the constitution for such a union should cover. Lafayette brought up the subject of slavery which troubled him deeply. He hoped the constitution would prohibit it.

The talk sometimes veered to Lafayette's personal life, in which Washington took fond interest. Lafayette had brought a portrait especially painted for Washington of his namesake, Georges, with Anastasie and Adrienne. It showed Adrienne holding a pint-size American uniform, Georges thrusting an arm into one sleeve and trying to get into the other one. With the painting came a letter from seven-year-old Anastasie in near-perfect English.

Surprised, Washington asked how she had learned the language. Lafayette explained that his children were taught English soon after they began to speak. The youngest, Virginie, at two, already used some English phrases. At "American dinners" in his Paris home in the Rue de Bourbon, Georges and Anastasie entertained guests with songs in English. The point of these dinners was to bring together visiting Americans or resident diplomats with influential French officials, hopefully as a means of helping to forward trade relationships between the two countries. From the age of four the Lafayette children were seated at such meals and were expected to answer in whichever tongue they might be addressed.

Time ticked on as the two men talked—much too fast to suit Lafayette. When he had to resume his tour, he left laden with smoked hams and preserves for Adrienne from Washington's wife, Martha. From Washington he carried a reply to Anastasie's letter. "I send you a kiss," the elder statesman wrote, "even though I fear it might be more agreeable to you if sent by a handsome American boy."

A sense of forboding depressed Lafayette as he said his good-byes. As his carriage rolled away, he wept. "I felt," he confided to his diary, "that I should never see that great man again." His intuition was right; this was his last visit with his revered commander. The affairs of his own country were to claim him totally until after Washington's death. Meanwhile, everywhere he went on this trip, he referred to himself as Washington's adopted son. And everywhere honors were heaped upon his head. New York, Connecticut, Maryland, Massachusetts and Virginia made him an honorary citizen. Harvard University awarded him a doctorate degree in law. When he left, a committee of the Continental Congress, composed of one member from each state, presented him with a congressional resolution of gratitude for his lobbying. His reply was a fervent hope for the future of America: "May this temple of freedom ever stand, a lesson to oppressors, an example to the oppressed, a sanctuary for the rights of mankind."

Except for the diary of the American visit, Lafayette's usually overflowing memoirs include surprisingly little information on this period of his life. His activities were mainly in the field of economics, and that was not a topic which fired his imagination. It is from Jefferson's acknowledgements of Lafayette's role in behalf of American commerce that his endeavors take shape. In a letter to John Jay, then American Secretary for Foreign Affairs, Jefferson wrote: "The assistance of M. de Lafayette in the whole of this business has been so earnest and so efficacious that I am duty bound to place it under the eye of Congress as worthy of their notice." Likewise, he wrote to John Adams, then representing the United States in England, "I have had . . . a most zealous and powerful auxiliary in the Marquis de Lafayette, by whose activity it has been sooner and better done than I could otherwise possibly have expected."

To James Madison, who was then working to organize a federal constitutional convention, Jefferson admitted that Lafayette's "education having been purely military, commerce was an unknown field to him. But," he added, "his good sense enabling him perfectly to comprehend whatever is explained to him, his agency has been very efficacious. He has a great deal of sound genius."

In token of his gratitude, Jefferson had a bust of Lafayette offered by the State of Virginia to the city of Paris and placed in City Hall. Carved by the French sculptor, Jean Houdon, who had also done busts of Jefferson, Franklin, John Paul Jones and Voltaire as well as a bust and a statue of Washington, it was the duplicate of a Lafayette bust Houdon had done for the Capitol at Richmond. With it came a letter from Jefferson who was ill and unable to attend the unveiling ceremony. The letter recalled the Virginia campaign.

> Their country was covered by a small army against a great one, their exhausted means supplied by his talents, their enemies finally forced to the spot whither their allies and confederates were collecting to relieve them . . . a war reduced . . . to where one blow should terminate it . . . and through the whole an implicit respect paid to the laws of the land.

Lafayette himself seems to have been touched by simpler plaudits. The fishermen of Nantucket sent him a resolution which he tucked into his memoirs:

> The generous concessions of the French government, obtained by the Marquis de Lafayette reanimates our sinking

industry, and fixes us upon this island, our antient [*sic*] home, from whence the new order of things was forcing us to emigrate. Penetrated with feelings of gratitude for such a service, the inhabitants of Nantucket . . . voted and resolved that each individual should give the milk of his cow for twenty-four hours, that the whole produce should be converted into a cheese weighing five hundred pounds, which should be sent to the Marquis de Lafayette, as a very feeble, in truth, but sincere testimony of the affection and gratitude of the inhabitants of Nantucket.

With the end of the trade campaign, Lafayette felt the need of a breathing spell. He returned to Chavaniac to find it in a bad state of disrepair. The stonework in the old chateau towers was crumbling; some of the floors were rotting. The grounds were ragged and the fields had been poorly tended. Chavaniac's foreman, anxious to restore standing in the face of his obvious neglect of duty, pointed out that the bins in the chateau granary were full—and this in a year of drought. His master could make a handsome profit selling the grain. "No," ordered Lafayette. "The villagers are hungry. Give it to them."

He threw himself into the work of restoring Chavaniac. Before he was finished, winter came. Snow encased the mountains and filled the valleys. Ice stilled the rivers. Lafayette holed up in his study, lighted the logs in the brick fireplace and set to work on two projects dear to his heart. One was an experiment in preparing slaves for emancipation; the other was a blueprint for a representative French government.

Immediately after the end of the American Revolution, Lafayette had started agitating, as he had done with Washington at Mount Vernon, for the prohibition of slavery in the United States. Even while lobbying in behalf of American trade needs, he found time to keep pressing for emancipation. To Jefferson he wrote, "I would never have drawn my sword in the cause of America, if I could have conceived that thereby I was founding a land of slavery." And somewhat later to John Adams:

> . . . in the cause of my black brethren I feel myself warmly interested, and most decidedly side, so far as respects them, against the white part of mankind. Whatever be the complexion of the enslaved, it does not, in my opinion, alter the complexion of the crime which the enslaver commits—a crime much blacker than any African face. It is to me a matter of great anxiety and concern to find that this trade is sometimes perpetrated under the flag of liberty, our dear and noble stripes, to which virtue and glory have been constant standard bearers.

To Washington, he proposed that the two of them buy a small estate "on which we may try the experiment to free Negroes and use them only as tenants." Finding Washington reluctant to join in this venture, he himself bought a plantation, *La Belle Gabrielle,* near Cayenne, in the French colony of Guiana. Having hired a manager to carry out his ideas, he now set about drawing up his instructions. The manager was to call all the slaves together and in their presence burn all the whips and other instruments of torture found on the place. He was to inform the slaves that Lafayette had bought them in order to prepare them for freedom, that blacks and whites were to be equally punished for violation of law, and equally rewarded for industry. Lafayette laid out a precise system of remuneration for work accomplished, with increments for exceptional endeavor. He provided for the establishment of a school. His aim was to prove to other planters in the colony that free men would work harder and better than slaves, and that their numbers would increase naturally by reproduction, thereby eliminating the need for the slave trade.

Evidently Lafayette's plan worked out, for a year later the French Minister of the Marine ordered the Intendant of

Cayenne to apply the same system on crown lands throughout the colony. And when, in the next decade, France abolished slavery in her West Indian colonies, only Guiana escaped the bloody uprisings which followed elsewhere.

The other project which occupied Lafayette in the winter of 1786–1787 was an adaptation for his own country of the principles which had drawn him to America. In his study, the gilt-framed mirror above the marble mantelpiece reflected, from the opposite wall, the Stuart portrait of Washington, the framed American Declaration of Independence, and next to it, an empty frame. From time to time Lafayette glanced up at the blank square. The document he was writing was to fill it. The time was drawing near now, he felt, when the French would be in need of a declaration of their own.

His sense of political timing was right. An emergency was on the way. In February a message came from the king. He had called an assembly of the nobility, high government officials, bishops and archbishops, who were known as the Notables. The Marquis was wanted immediately at Versailles. He was to be assigned to the section headed by the king's younger brother, the Count d'Artois. The gentlemen were welcomed by Calonne with a long confession on the state of the public treasury. For almost three hundred years, French kings (with one outstanding exception, Henry IV) had spent with increasing lavishness and without the slightest attention to balancing income and outgo. The present Louis XVI was no exception to this pattern. The flat truth, which Calonne revealed to the Notables, was that the country was now dead broke. What to do about it?

The minister set forth several suggestions, which in that time—the late eighteenth century—that place—the palace of Versailles—and to that audience—one hundred forty of the most privileged aristocracy of the realm—were revolutionary. "Only in the abolition of abuses," he began, "lies the means to answer our needs. The abuses we must today wipe out in order to restore public health are those of the widest extent, enjoying the most protection."

He went on to propose six reforms: the establishment of provincial assemblies, a land tax, a tax on clergy, a revision of the poll tax, freedom of trade in grains, a system of rents to be substituted for forced labor in return for land use.

After his speech the shocked aristocrats broke up into their assigned sections. In the d'Artois group, Lafayette rose to make a proposal: convoke an assembly that would include the *people* of France and put to them the question of bankruptcy. A sharp dialogue ensued.

"What, are you asking for a States-General?" demanded an incredulous d'Artois. The States-General was a parliamentary group which grew out of the king's council in the late Middle Ages. It met at the pleasure of the monarch—a pleasure in which no monarchs had indulged for one hundred and seventy-six years at the time Lafayette made his suggestion.

"Yes, sir," Lafayette replied to d'Artois.

D'Artois still couldn't believe his ears. "You mean you desire that I should take in writing and report to the king that the motion to convoke the States-General has been made by the Marquis de Lafayette?"

"Yes, sir," Lafayette repeated, "and something more." He went on to support all Calonne's proposals and to ask in addition for abolition of *lettres de cachet,* and for an end to discrimination against Protestants.

The assemblage broke up without any agreement on this or other action, but Lafayette was optimistic that it was only a beginning and that the beginning would, as he wrote George Washington, "lead to great good." He was particularly enthusiastic about Calonne's regional assemblies idea. "Calonne deserves the country's gratitude for having chosen this road," he added.

Evidently the king did not agree. Calonne was fired. In the

salons, the smart set coined an Anglo-French play on words to jeer at the incompetence of the assembly. *Not-Able,* they called it. Across the country, the people, weary of talk, began taking matters in their own hands. They led protest marches to Paris, which got several of them thrown into the Bastille, the city's dreaded state prison. They staged riots at home. The thrust of their drive was for the calling of the States-General which Lafayette had proposed to the astounded brother of the king. The meeting had indeed been a beginning, but the beginning of a reverse of what Lafayette envisioned. Rather it was the vision of Samuel Cooper that waited its cue in the wings.

# 4

## *Man in the Middle*

THE French historian, Alexis de Tocqueville, recreating sixty-seven years later the events leading up to the 1789 French Revolution, wrote: "By destroying a part of the institutions of the Middle Ages, men made a hundred times more odious those which they allowed to remain." The "torrents" of blood which Cooper had warned against, and toward which the tide of public opinion was propelling France in 1787, were the result of rising expectations rather than depressed conditions. That the group of protesters thrown into the Bastille was able to string newly invented arc lights around its turrets as a gesture of defiance shows how little basis existed at that time for the Bastille's gruesome reputation. But its creaking drawbridges, its gloomy battlements were hated symbols. They stood for a vanishing feudalism, an organization of society from the top down, that was not vanishing fast enough to suit the generation of the Enlightenment.

The disciples of the Enlightenment included in their fold not only the aristocrats with whom the philosophy was the "in" thing, intellectually, but a great portion of the middle class, the *bourgeoisie.* The bourgeois read the same books and journals as the aristocrats; they spoke the same elegant tongue. A good many were as rich—and some were richer than those who rated titles. Yet they did not share the same privileges. The gulf between the two classes of society boiled with bourgeois resentment—sometimes over petty but aggravating distinctions, such as hunting and fishing rights—sometimes over weighted injustice, such as a tax system which restricted most exemptions to men of noble birth.

The bloodshed about to break might have been avoided if, as in eighteenth-century England, the peers, despite their rank, had been subject to the same system of justice as any other people, and enjoyed no greater privileges than any other. But they chose to cling to their privileges and the king chose to support them. Had he sided with the people, the monarchy might have survived. The people did not intend, in the beginning, to do away with it. On the contrary, they were ready to grant their king all powers important for the conduct of a fair and just government, provided *they* did the granting rather than the other way around, and provided they kept a voice equal to their numbers in the resulting system of government.

Consequently Lafayette's motion for a meeting of the States-General struck a responsive chord across the country. Near bankruptcy, the king was forced to call such a meeting when the Parlement refused to approve two new taxes he requested. Having sniffed the wind, the Parlement declared that "only the nation assembled in the States-General can give the consent necessary."

As originally constituted, the States, or houses, were three: the clergy, nobility and commons, each representing their own class of society, each with an equal number of delegates. The houses met separately but conferred until a single vote could be cast by all three. Commons represented twenty-five million people. Nobles and clergy combined represented two hundred and fifty thousand. Yet together they had twice as many votes as commons or the Third Estate, as it was often known.

Obviously, commons was disadvantaged. The representatives refused to meet until the king promised that they could have the same number of votes as nobles and clergy put together. In the meanwhile Lafayette, de Lauzon, his brother-in-law de Noailles, and a group of senior statesmen and historians, nobles all, had formed La Société de Trente, the Society of Thirty, to support within the Assembly an equalization of voting power.

The members often dined at Lafayette's home. Like the American dinners he had hosted during the campaign for French-American trade, these dinners had a purpose. Plans were laid to achieve the Society's purpose: an equalization of voting power. On all such occasions, Adrienne was an accomplished hostess. Whether or not she completely agreed with her husband's goals, she made them hers and defended them well. What he wanted, she wanted for him. So much of his life was so far apart from hers that she treasured those occasions when her efforts were essential to him. "I am Fayettist," she liked to say. It was her declaration of love.

One reservation she had. She felt that the high-keyed atmosphere of the household, the group comings and goings, distracted the attention of her son from his studies. Quietly, she leased separate lodgings nearby where Georges and his tutor, Felix Frestel, could work uninterrupted. He would have plenty of time later to enlist in causes.

The Lafayette dinners helped make the cause fashionable. Combined with other forces, it created such pressure that Louis agreed to give commons what they wanted. But not without a trick up his sleeve. When the Estates met at Versailles on May 5, 1789, they found themselves quartered in separate chambers, according to the ancient custom. No longer need they agree on a single vote for all three chambers, but each was expected to cast only one unit vote. This system meant, of course, that the Third Estate's one vote could still be overruled by the two contrary votes of the clergy and nobles. Such was Louis's trick.

Commons invited the clergy and nobles to join them and to vote as individuals. One hundred forty-three priests and six bishops accepted the invitation; so did a handful of nobles. For Lafayette, response to the invitation posed a problem. He distrusted unicameral, or one house legislatures, having seen the failure of one in Pennsylvania. Furthermore, he had been elected to the States-General by the nobility of Auvergne, and he was under strict command from his electors to vote with his own order, the house of nobles. He sought Jefferson's advice. The American statesman's reply went straight to the point: "Your instructions are . . . a difficulty which a single effort will surmount. Your instructions can never embarrass you a second time, whereas an acquiescence under them will produce greater difficulties every day, and without end."

But Jefferson was more concerned about his friend's problem than his brief answer would indicate. To Washington he described his feelings in some detail:

> I am in great pain for the Marquis de Lafayette. His principles you know are clearly with the people; but having been elected for the Noblesse of Auvergne, they have laid him under express instructions to vote . . . by orders and not persons. This would ruin him with the Tiers État, and it is not possible he could continue long to give satisfaction to the Noblesse. I have not hesitated to press on him to burn his instructions and follow his conscience . . . If he cannot effect a conciliatory plan, he will surely take his stand manfully at once with the Tiers État.

While Lafayette was debating the question with himself, a rapid succession of circumstances took the decision out of his hands. The Third Estate, their membership swelled by some representatives from the other houses, declared themselves to be the entirety of the States-General, or, as they rephrased the name, the National Assembly. The king closed the hall in which they were meeting. Unperturbed, they moved to the *jeu de paume,* an inside tennis court nearby. There they took an oath to stay together until they should have drawn up a constitution for the kingdom. Confronted with that action, the fund-starved Louis gave in and ordered the nobles and clergy to meet with commons in one chamber. Lafayette was saved from choice. The joint assembly voted that taxes should continue to be collected only so long as the members continued to sit, thus protecting itself from another royal effort to cut off parliamentary discussion.

The document with which this first French National Assembly commenced the task of drawing up a constitution was the one which Lafayette had started to compose the preceding January in his Chavaniac study. During the three months between the meeting of the Notables and the convening of the States-General he returned to Chavaniac. There, with a great deal of editorial help from Thomas Jefferson, with whom he was in constant correspondence, he worked feverishly to complete his presentation.

Spring arrived as his quill filled page after page with his cramped, angular handwriting. When occasionally he looked up from his task as he discarded one sheet and began another anew, he could see from his study window the budding gorse begin to gild his greening fields. Far off, the melting snows uncapped the mountain peaks. Later he recalled having been conscious of the change and linking it with the "natural life" he was trying to bring forth for France. "Liberty," he said, "is the natural state of being for mankind." But during those months devoted to defining liberty in political practice, he indulged in little reverie. Wholly absorbed in his endeavor, he pursued it alone. He had left Adrienne in Paris. Only through Jefferson did she receive news of him.

Jefferson, meanwhile, was sharing the mass of copy with others. He sent James Madison the Bill of Rights with which Lafayette's declaration opened. "You will see," Jefferson wrote, "that it contains the essential principles of ours, adapted as much as could be to the essential state of things here." As the work progressed Jefferson made frequent suggestions for change, most of which Lafayette was glad to use. For example, Jefferson proposed clear separation of legislative, executive and judicial powers; he deleted from Lafayette's list of man's "inalienable rights" the phrase "the safeguarding of . . . honor" as smacking too much of aristocratic fantasy for a republican constitution. One principle, regarding property rights, which Jefferson would have preferred to see omitted, Lafayette insisted on retaining. Property rights were not, in Jefferson's mind, inalienable. To Lafayette they were. He was a revolutionary, but not a radical. His concept of the meaning of free government was never as far-reaching as that of his mentor.

He introduced his declaration in the Assembly on July 11, 1789. Up until the day before he was still asking for and incorporating Jefferson's suggestions.* As finally adopted by the Assembly on August 26th, the Declaration of Rights of Man and the Citizens first states the conviction that the "purpose of government" is to safeguard the "natural and inalienable rights of man." It defines these rights as "liberty, property, safety and resistance to oppression." These are further spelled out by guarantees of citizen participation in making "laws which must apply equally to all," and in "fixing the amounts of taxes and means of collecting them." Also included is the right to "speak, write and print with freedom, being responsible, however, for such abuses of freedom as shall be defined by law"; the right not to be "disquieted on account of . . . opinions, including . . . religious views, provided that they do not disturb the public order established by law"; the right "not to be accused, arrested or imprisoned,

---

* The Library of Congress in Washington, D.C. has a draft in Lafayette's handwriting which contains some of these suggestions in marginal notes written by Jefferson.

except in the cases and according to the forms prescribed by law, and the right "to be held innocent until . . . declared guilty" by due process of law. Other provisions cover the several responsibilities of branches of government and the administration of the army for the purpose of "guarding the rights of man and the citizen."

In releasing the document for public print, the Assembly claimed, with good reason, that the "rights of man, misconceived and insulted for centuries" were "reestablished for all humanity in this declaration which shall serve as an everlasting war cry against oppressors." With the English Magna Carta, which in 1215 made English monarchs subject to law, and the American Bill of Rights, the French Declaration of the Rights of Man and the Citizen stands as one of Western civilization's three most enlightened spellings-out of the requirements for a free, but organized society. It became the basis not only for a French constitution, but for similar statements of law in other European nations. And although France has drawn up numerous constitutions since Lafayette's time, all those which were democratic, including the present one, reflect the Declaration of which Lafayette was the prime mover.

The long weeks between the July introduction of the Declaration and its August passage offered nothing to calm the restlessness of the people which had been steadily mounting since June, when Louis had dismissed Finance Minister Necker. Necker had returned to office as the second to fill the post after the firing of Calonne. No man, however gifted, seemed to meet Louis's requirements—all of which could be summed up in two words: more money. Necker was a moderate man with a good grasp of the nation's problems. The people liked him and were incensed by his dismissal. They draped a bust of him in black and paraded it through the streets. Louis, daily more fearful of their mood, and distrusting his French guards, many of whom openly proclaimed allegiance to the Third Estate, hired Swiss and German soldiers to protect the royal family. This move outraged Paris. A mob showered the foreign troops with stones.

As the weather grew hotter, so did the tempers of the people. By July, antiroyalist pamphlets were rolling in the hundreds from printing presses. Street-corner speakers with rumors as texts, whipped up public ire. "The foreign troops are about to butcher the patriots" . . . "the brigands are marching on Paris," such were the imaginary evils reported from one end of the city to the other.

Meanwhile the Assembly was elatedly introducing, discussing, amending and perfecting the Declaration. The Assembly delegates were working with the prospect of change; the people saw no change. They wanted action. Daily in the gardens of the Palais Royal, a fiery young pamphleteer and law student, Camille Desmoulins, egged them on. On the day after the introduction of the Declaration, July 12th, orating atop a chair, he picked a leaf from a horse chestnut tree above him and fashioned a cockade which he stuck in his hair. His audience forced all passers-by to do likewise. Those who hesitated were pummeled. The crowd was beginning to sense its power. At the strategic moment Desmoulins cried "To arms!" and the crowd surged to the shops of gunsmiths, stripping the shelves.

The next day, and the next, they stripped government arsenals of cannon. Most of the powder, it was rumored, had been taken to the Bastille, from which an attack was to be launched on Paris. "To the Bastille! To the Bastille!" The cry swelled like a cresting wave through the crowd. It had become a mob. The march was on.

At the gates of the Bastille, a guardsman leading the marchers demanded admission for all. The prison's governor, de Launay, refused the demand, but offered to let a committee come in to see that no attack was being prepared. The mob's response was to fire a cannon they had dragged to the prison walls. The siege was brief but bloody. Some one hundred of the attackers were killed. The remainder took their revenge by slaughtering the garrison defending the Bastille, beheading de Launay and another officer and parading their heads, mounted on pikes, through the streets of Paris. In the cells they found only seven prisoners. These they released.

The National Assembly was horrified at the violence. Heavily representative of the bourgeoisie, the members were men of property, strictly on the side of law and order. Quickly they organized a volunteer National Guard to keep order. Although meant to calm the people, this step also restrained the king. It prevented him from seizing the Bastille march as an excuse to send out his own soldiers. Lafayette was appointed Commander-in-Chief of the Guard and elected Vice-President of the Assembly. The two positions combined made him the strongest man in France. They also cast him in opposing roles. As a legislator, he was working for the suppression of privileged ranks (with the exception of the royal family) and equality of all citizens. As a soldier, his responsibility was to suppress the excesses of the people. No one was more conscious of his dilemma than Lafayette himself. On July 16th, two days after the sack of the Bastille, he reflected in his journal:

> The people in its [*sic*] delirium can only be kept quiet by myself. Forty thousand souls assemble, the excitement is at its height; I appear and a word from me disperses them. I have already saved the lives of six persons who were to be hanged . . . but this maddened people will not listen to me always. My position is unlike anyone else's; I am king in Paris, but it is over an angry people.

His statement was prophetic. More and more, as the Revolution progressed, his responsibility for preventing "delirium" from undermining revolutionary gains would increase. And the more he found it necessary to use force to prevent force, the less influence his presence would exert on "an angry people."

Trying to create order out of disorder, he felt singularly alone. He desperately wanted the discipline of his guards to grow from within, to spring from their understanding of their duties rather than from his decree. His soldiers were all volunteers, without any previous experience in military discipline. It would take time for an esprit de corps to develop. Yet there was no time. Not only were the people already out of hand; they were being still further aroused by radicals who had goals far easier to attain than Lafayette's—these radicals were flattering the mobs in order to grasp power for themselves.

Meanwhile, a great part of the Assembly was crying that the first and foremost task of the realm was to uphold the law—while another part, some of Lafayette's close friends, the Lameth brothers among them, were busily organizing revolutionary clubs to overthrow the Assembly's law-and-order majority. Both groups expected the support of Lafayette and his unorganized guards.

It was all very well, back in the days of the Virginia campaign in the United States, for Lafayette to have written Jefferson that the "inconveniences" of "popular government" were "compensated by [its] numberless blessings." Then Jefferson carried the final responsibility for the fate of the state; now no buffer stood between Lafayette and the destiny of his ideal.

A few days after his appointment as Commander of the Guards, a priest was being attacked by a crowd in the square in front of City Hall. Why? The precise reason had been lost in the mounting mob fury. Coincidentally, Lafayette had asked Frestel to bring ten-year-old Georges to meet him at City Hall. Taking the boy in his arms, he went out onto the balcony and holding Georges up high where he could be seen, he distracted the mob's attention by calling, *"Messieurs, j'ai l'honneur de vous présenter mon fils."* Gentlemen, I have the honor to introduce my son to you. During the utter surprise with which this action stunned the mob, Lafayette had the unfortunate priest hustled to safety inside.

On another occasion his balcony techniques were less successful. A rumor had arisen concerning one of the king's ministers, Joseph Foulon. He was a member of a group known as the "Queen's Party," die-hard monarchists who were urging Louis not to surrender an iota of royal authority. Word was passed that Foulon was cornering wheat. Paris was short of bread at that point—and bread to the French was then, as it is now, not merely the so-called staff of life, but the staff of the soul. Food without it was not, is not, a meal. Not only was Foulon supposedly hoarding wheat, he was also said to have remarked, "The people ought to be happy to be given straw to eat."

A mob appointed itself as the arm of justice and dragged him to City Hall. There Lafayette confronted the vigilantes. "I am known to you all," he said. "You have made me your commander . . . I must speak to you with all the liberty and frankness for which I am known . . . I insist that the law be respected, that law, without which there can be no liberty, without which I . . . cannot share in this revolution. I command that this man be taken . . . to trial."

His words were drowned in the mob's roar. Lafayette repeated the message. For minutes the contest between the commander and the people continued. The third time Lafayette spoke, the mob quieted. Someone applauded him. The applause, like the roaring, was contagious. All hands began to clap.

Lafayette would have won the victory had it not been for Foulon himself. The minister made the fatal mistake of joining in the applause. Those standing close to him called out, "Look, look! Foulon and Lafayette have an understanding!"

The supposition passed from mouth to mouth. The mob dragged him out of the City Hall and butchered him in the street. Then they sought out his son-in-law and hacked him to death with a hundred strokes of a sword.

That night they paraded the heads of their victims on pikes and as they knocked the two together, they yelled, "Kiss papa, kiss papa." The American patriot, Gouveneur Morris, then in France negotiating a tobacco deal, observed the scene from his window. "Gracious God! What a people!" he wrote home.

Lafayette resigned as commander. "The people have not listened to my advice," he said. "The day in which they fail in their trust in me, I must leave a post in which I can no longer be of use." The outcry at his resignation was universal. The mob, once so sure of itself, was suddenly frightened. The guard was in disarray. The Assembly was appalled. Under pressure, Lafayette consented to remain in his post. But he attached a condition. "Every citizen must take a solemn oath to maintain justice and public order." Conscience-stricken, the people took the oath meekly enough. For the time being calm prevailed in Paris.

The story was different in the rest of the country. In the provinces, complete anarchy took over. The king's authority was dead; the authority of the National Assembly was not yet born. Each town, each village took the law into its own hands, sacking, burning, slaughtering. "Anarchy," the Venetian Ambassador wrote sarcastically home, "is the first aspect of the regeneration it is desired to bestow on France."

What to do? The Viscount de Noailles, Lafayette's brother-in-law, understood the situation well. "The sole cause of this agitation," he declared, "is the retention of feudal rights, and the sole remedy is to abolish them."

The nature of these rights had been clearly spelled out in the *cahiers* which the Assembly had collected. These were kingdom-wide lists of citizens' grievances. A principal sore-point among them was the land privileges of aristocratic land holders. Although most of the large landholdings in France had been broken up and sold piecemeal, fees still had to be paid to whoever lived in the manor house, whether or not the occupant was an heir of the original owner. Cattle driven past the manorhouse were taxed. The only community bake-ovens and winepresses were owned by the manor lord, and those using these facilities were forced to pay off with a percentage of wine and bread.

Every lord kept four or five thousand pigeons for sport hunting, and an equal number of deer and rabbits were allowed to run wild. Only the lord was privileged to shoot these nuisances which ate farmers' seeds or consumed young crops. Whenever a piece of estate land was sold, one fifth of the proceeds went to the lord. There were other grievances: the enormous, tax-free wealth of the church, forced tithing, exemptions from military service and taxes for nobility, a hated tax on salt, the poll tax, press censorship, *lettres de cachet*. Some of these wrongs were already being corrected by the Declaration of Rights of Man and the Citizen; others were covered as it was amended, or were abolished by decree. Nobles like de Noailles rose in the Assembly voluntarily to give up their privileges. Young apostles of the Enlightenment vied with each other to forfeit hunting rights and monopolies. Cardinals and archbishops relinquished tithes. With a sudden burst of speed, France seemed well on the way to becoming a nation of citizens with equally inalienable rights. "A people bent under the yoke once again walks erect," exulted the Count de Ségur.

To assure nationwide impact for its legislation, the Assembly changed the map of France. The provinces had habitually conducted their affairs much like separate kingdoms. For the provinces the Assembly substituted administrative districts, or *departements* of the national government, the same departments into which France is today divided. These were in turn subdivided into cantons and finally communes, municipal governments. Thus were the reforms made in Paris guaranteed also to the rest of the country. Burning and sacking of the countryside subsided as central authority moved in.

The form of national government proposed by the Declaration was a constitutional monarchy. It put the monarchy at the service of the people as represented by their elected assembly. Louis was no longer King of France, but King of the French and not only by "the Grace of God," but by "the Constitutional law of the State." The National Assembly appointed a committee to draw up a constitution based on the principles of the Declaration. When the committee reported back to the Assembly, a clause-by-clause debate of the constitution began. The voice of the vice-president, Lafayette, was frequently heard. For him, the American Constitution was, with the exception of the powers of the president, which he felt were too great, the perfect model. Time and again he cited it, particularly with reference to a bicameral legislature, which the committee had not recommended and which most of the Assembly opposed. His reference to the two American houses and other features of his model were so repetitive that whenever he rose to his feet, his fellow legislators took to sighing, *"Ah, l'Amerique!"*

At that stage of the Revolution, Lafayette was engaged in reform on two fronts. As a legislator, he was midwifing a new concept of French law; as a soldier, a new concept of the French military. He was trying to model into a reliable armed force a group of volunteers who were so independent that they frequently refused duty in the rain. From his American army experience he knew that volunteers were best trained by professional leaders, men like de Kalb and von Steuben, for example. Yet arbitrary hiring of professionals would cut across the grain of the spirit of the times which leaned over backwards in demanding total equality—even in the army. Lafayette could not impose trained and salaried professional officers on his men. The men would have to want them. His solution was to insist on such a rigorous work schedule that the guards became more than willing to have paid professionals lift some of the load.

Once over this hump, he presented to the Commune of Paris his plans for organization of the guard. With him he brought the ornamental cockade he had designed as their emblem. It was red, white and blue. "I bring you," he said to the mayor, "a cockade which will go round the world, and an institution both civil and military which will triumph over the ancient tactics of Europe and which will conquer arbitrary governments which do not imitate our example." He clothed his soldiers in red, white and blue uniforms and issued to the regiments the tricolor flag which became and remained the nation's flag.

His choice of color combination may have been subconsciously influenced by the American colors, but his conscious reasoning, a stroke of genius, was purely political. The colors of Paris, red and blue, had been adopted as the colors of the Revolution. But they were also the colors of the Duke D'Orléans, who pretended sympathy with the revolutionaries but who, Lafayette rightly suspected, cherished the ambition to seize the throne for himself. Under these circumstances, Lafayette considered the red and blue a dangerous association. White, on the other hand, was the traditional color of French royalty. By combining it with the revolution's red and blue, he suggested the idea of a constitutional monarchy toward which the Assembly was working. And his soldiers with their flags, their cockades and their uniforms were given an identity with that goal. An esprit de corps began to form.

"I am in the midst of a great adventure," Lafayette wrote to George Washington, enclosing in his letter the keys of the Bastille. His exuberance had returned. He needed it. The road ahead was rocky. The Assembly soon became clutched in the throes of debate over whether the Constitution should give the monarch the power to veto actions of the Assembly. The leader of the pro-veto forces was the wisest of the revolutionaries, a nobleman, Honoré, Count de Mirabeau, who had gotten himself elected delegate to the Third Estate from the southern city of Aix-en-Provence and had been a member of the Society of Thirty. He was one of the few who understood the need for checks and balances in government. "When you undertake to run a revolution, the difficulty is not to make it go" he said. "It is to hold it in check." He added that the representatives could themselves "constitute an aristocracy dangerous to freedom. It is against this aristocracy that the veto is needed. The representatives would likewise have their veto which would lie in the refusal to vote taxes."

The leaders of the anti-veto forces were the fanatic physician-scientist and apostle of violence, Jean Paul Marat, and the Duke d'Orléans. The Duke's agents warned all over Paris, "The king will veto and you will have no bread." Marat attacked Lafayette, also Mirabeau and the pro-veto forces as "traitors." Between them, Marat and the Duke rearoused the populace, which had been relatively law-abiding since the butchering of Foulon and the threatened resignation of Lafayette. Now, however, made fearful by propaganda, the people were finding the oath of obedience to law which Lafayette had exacted difficult to keep. Promising had been easier than performing and the street talk took on a threatening tone.

How about that flour supposedly cached at Versailles? Why not confiscate it? Combine the act with a march on the Assembly at Versailles to throw out the wealthy bourgeois who was its president, at the same time hauling from the throne the *Autrichienne,* that Austrian woman, who was said to have trampled upon the tricolor.

Within the Assembly, too, the debates grew stormier. Anxious to preserve order, Lafayette, who was privately pro-veto, publicly straddled the issue. In an apparently neutral position himself, he sought to bring together some of the more reasonable legislators on both sides of the question in an atmosphere removed from the fuming in the Assembly. He hoped that, thus accommodated, they could work out among themselves a compromise which they could later persuade the others to accept. For this purpose he invited them to dine at Jefferson's house—without consulting Jefferson in advance. On the day before the dinner, he dropped Jefferson a hasty note:

My dear friend,

I beg for liberty's sake you will break every engagement to give us a dinner tomorrow wenesday [*sic*]. We shall be some members of the National Assembly—eight of us whom I want to coalize as being the only means to prevent a total dissolution and civil war. The difficulty between us is the King's veto. . . . If they don't agree in a few days, we shall have no great majority in favor of any plan and it must end in a war. . . . The discontented party will unite either with aristocratic or factious people. The gentlemen wish to consult you and me; they will dine tomorrow at your house, as mine is always full. I depend on you to receive us . . . I think this dinner is of an immediate and great importance.

Adieu my dear friend,<br>L.f.

Tuesday.

Evidently it did not occur to Lafayette that Jefferson might find the situation acutely embarrassing, as indeed he did. He already refused an invitation from the Archbishop of Bordeaux, Chairman of the Assembly's Constitutional Committee, to aid that committee. Having acknowledged the honor done him by the request, he had pointed out that as an official representative of the United States in France, he could not legitimately intervene in French governmental affairs. But, as

Lafayette had intended, he received Lafayette's note too late to refuse without seeming discourteous, perhaps even seeming to slight members of the Assembly. There was no time for the excuse he had given the Archbishop of Bordeaux. He solved the problem by reporting the entire dinner conversation to the French Foreign Minister the next morning, with apologies and an explanation of his situation.

According to Jefferson's account, the discussion, which went on for six hours, concluded with "agreement on mutual sacrifices" which gave the anti-veto representatives sufficient assurance to persuade their comrades to accept the veto, while supplying the pro-veto forces with an assurance of victory they could not have otherwise obtained. In sum, the king could use the veto power over any measure passed by the Assembly, but he was strictly prohibited from dissolving it and since the Assembly could also, according to Mirabeau's prescription, refuse him funds whenever they wished to bring him to terms, the representatives kept the upper hand. Their hand was further reinforced by a provision preventing the royal army from coming any closer to their meeting place than thirty miles. They could not be stormed by a stubborn or irate monarch. The fact that the right to vote for representatives was limited to taxpayers reassured conservatives that, despite the Assembly's upper hand, it would be unlikely to propose measures harmful to bourgeois bank accounts.

The propaganda of Marat and Orléans over the veto threat might have been nullified by the agreement made at Jefferson's dinner table, had it not been for the stupidity of Louis XVI. He refused to ratify the Declaration of Rights. His refusal, added to the propaganda, and to rumors about flour and the trampling of the tricolor, triggered the street crowds. Off to Versailles to capture the flour, butcher the queen, get rid of the Assembly president! The motives of the marchers varied, but they all agreed on forcing Lafayette to accompany them. It would be a test of his loyalty to their cause.

They began congregating at guard headquarters on the morning of October 5th. All day long, Lafayette argued with them. "Strange," was the reply shouted back at him, "that Lafayette should wish to command the people, when it is for the people to command Lafayette." His own guardsmen took the people's side. He saw that the work of months hung in the balance. *"À Versailles ou à la lanterne!"* the mob howled. To Versailles or be strung up. He did not fear the hanging—he feared the destruction of his work, of the work of the Assembly, of a positive outcome for so many positive labors. He compromised. In return for their oath of allegiance to the throne, he agreed to come with his haranguers. He had scant trust in the oath—the second such he had administered—for he was learning that "the common man," the god of his adolescence, could be as unpredictable, and at times as cruel, as the absolute monarchy he was dedicated to elasticizing. Yet it was better to go with them than to let them go alone. His would at least be one restraining presence.

"He rode at the head of his troops like a criminal led to a slaughter," an eye witness recorded. Once at Versailles he responded automatically to crisis. Having had their way in forcing him to accompany them, the marchers gave him complete freedom of action. First he found the Assembly president and assured him that he had come to protect the king and queen and the process of law. Next he went to the palace. The entrance foyer was filled with disturbed courtiers. "Look at Cromwell!" one of them called out, referring to an English revolutionary of the preceding century whose success depended heavily on his comrades-at-arms. Lafayette stopped in midstride. "Sir," he replied, contempt icing his voice, "Cromwell would not have acted alone."

He roused the king and persuaded him to dismiss from the courtyard all but a few of the foreign bodyguards whom the people loathed. He replaced them with his own National Guard. The mob fired on the remaining bodyguards, killing two and wounding others. A yelling mass poured into the courtyard. Then it was that he roused the queen and took her to the balcony to confront the subjects screaming for her thighs and liver.

"Those moments on the balcony," Lafayette recalled many years later, "were worth more than the twenty-four hours of talking which had preceded them." He had slaked the thirst for blood. But to do so, he had again to make some compromise. The mob insisted that the royal family return to Paris with them, and that thereafter the Assembly should meet in Paris, where the people could keep an eye on it, rather than in Versailles. A small group started back to Paris, carrying like banners the piked heads of the slain bodyguards. The rest followed in the late afternoon, with the few sacks of flour they had found, the king, queen and their son in tow. "The baker, the baker's wife and the baker's boy," they called their captives.

They reached City Hall at 9:00 P.M. Once more Lafayette staged a balcony scene with the rulers. Toward the end, rain began to fall again. The king, queen and dauphin were driven to the Tuileries Palace, which was euphemistically to be the royal residence—in reality the royal prison. To the Count d'Estaing, Lafayette's erstwhile ally in the American Revolution, now among his copatriots in the French struggle for liberty, Lafayette said, "This night's events are almost enough to turn me into a royalist." Almost, but not quite. He was neither for royalty nor for the mob. He knew what he was against: despotism, whether royal or popular. He had yet to find the French way to keep one from leading to the other. If the Americans could do it, why couldn't the French?

This was the long-term problem. Another that threatened immediately, he handled with immediacy. At Versailles he had glimpsed the Duke d'Orléans moving among the mob in the courtyard. Two days afterward he called on the Duke with a brief warning. "Sir," he said, "I have been more responsible than anyone for breaking the steps that lead to the throne; the nation has put the king on the last step; I shall keep him there despite you, and before you take his place, you will have to pass over my body, a difficult thing to do."

Indeed, difficult. Lafayette's conduct through the night of October 5th and the day of October 6th had reinforced the people's admiration for him, and the trust of officials as well. The king ratified the Declaration and on February 4, 1790, attended a session of the Assembly to announce his acceptance of the principles of the revolution. He promised also "to prepare the mind and heart" of his son and heir "for the new order of things which circumstances have brought about."

Another period of calm ensued. The Assembly went about its business in the riding school of the Tuileries. The behavior of the lawmakers, however, was not such as to inspire confidence in the minds of leaders like Lafayette and Mirabeau. The members lacked political education; they knew very little about parliamentary procedures. Sessions were disorderly and very often interrupted by onlookers in the packed galleries. Bringing the Assembly to Paris where deliberations could be subjected to such pressures had been a mistake. Little by little, the real power of government began to pass from the Assembly to outside political clubs whose representatives in the Assembly voted in blocs in accordance with decisions made at club meetings. In representing their clubs, they lost sight of their obligation to represent their constituents.

The earliest of these clubs—and the one which would eventually become the most powerful—was the Jacobins, of which Mirabeau was a leader. The Feuillants, organized later, were composed largely of Lafayette's followers. At first the Jacobins were moderates; their political philosophy was constitutional monarchy. But after the death of Mirabeau in 1791, they turned to advocating abolition of the throne and were responsible for launching the bloodiest years of the revolution.

The Girondists, a third club, most of whose members came from the Department of the Gironde around the city of Bordeaux, were moderates who split off from the Jacobins as the latter began to lose their moderate tone. The fourth, the Cordeliers, were outright radicals from the start. Eventually they combined with radical elements in the moderate clubs to form what was called "the Mountain," because the seats of their Assemblymen were the highest in the riding school.

If there was one thing above all others that revolutionary France, with its feeble grasp on unity, *didn't* need, that one thing was the rivalry among these clubs for political control. The rivalry was like grease on the reins of government. The Assembly gradually began to lose its grip. Under the double pressure of need for money and the ambition to out-revolutionize the more revolutionary elements in the chamber, moderates in the Assembly joined radicals in passing legislation that violated a key principle of the declaration, the principle of freedom of religion. Under the terms of the new law, church property was seized by the state, priests and prelates were made employees of the state, salaried by the state and forced to take an oath of allegiance to the state or do without pay.

The bishops of France, with the exception of four, refused to take the oath and a great number of priests followed their example. Many earnest citizens who recognized the need for church reform, but who did not believe the church of God should be dependent on government by man, were antagonized. Numbers of them left the country. With them went others who wanted nothing to do with any part of the revolution. The latter, known as *emigrés,* began to plot with Austria and Prussia to attack France and restore the French monarchy.

Moreover, the seizing of church property proved no remedy for the country's economic ills. With church lands as security, the Assembly issued paper money known as assignats. These soon proved worthless. So much land had been thrown so suddenly on the market that real estate prices nose-dived and the value of the paper money's security was all but wiped out. Unemployment set in. The Cordeliers, supported by a few of the Jacobins were quick to exploit the people's dissatisfaction. They encouraged and helped organize strikes which further dislocated the unstable economy, which produced further dissatisfaction; this they encouraged the people to express in riots. Together with the Duke d'Orléans, who played with them for tactical reasons, they even tried to stir up mutiny in the National Guard. They hoped to render it incapable of coping with the riots.

For a while, they hoped in vain. Lafayette was almost always on the scene with his troops. One of the daily journals carried a story of his personal intervention with a mob trying to string up some wretch who had stolen a sack of oats. When the queen read it, she commented, "Odd that the little redhead should forever by trying to save everyone except kings." Lafayette had spent many hours with her and her husband trying to convince them that their acceptance of constitutional monarchy, their cooperation with the Assembly, would be the only means of saving the throne. In the course of these discussions, Marie was at least honest with Lafayette. She made no pretense of accepting the idea of a constitution; she openly despised the Assembly and she didn't bother to disguise her contempt for Lafayette himself. The king, on the other hand, while negotiating with both Lafayette and Mirabeau and pretending to accept the principles of the Revolution, was secretly plotting to escape and enlist Austrian, Prussian and emigré aid in recovering an unfettered throne.

At the same time that Lafayette was trying to reeducate the royal family, he was attempting to persuade some of his Jacobin friends like the Lameth brothers to tone down their activities. The result was that both extremes detested him equally. *"Motier, l'un, motier l'autre,"* he was dubbed in a play of his own name, Motier and *moitié,* the French word for half. Half one, half the other.

The day of February 28, 1791, was a day which silhouetted the double antagonisms aroused by this man in the middle. A royalist plot had been hatched to draw Lafayette to the fortress of Vincennes, at the opposite end of Paris from the Tuileries, and keep him engaged there while a group of courtiers carried the royal family from the Tuileries to the city of Peronne. Accordingly, agents instigated a mob to march on Vincennes. As soon as Lafayette heard news of the march he hastened to the fort with his guards, arrested the leaders of the mob, and, by threatening to use his artillery, restored order in Saint Antoine, the district surrounding Vincennes. The royalist plan had also included assassination of Lafayette. That part of the plot miscarried, the hired assassin, firing hurriedly and from a distance, mistook Lafayette's aide-de-camp for him. Lafayette's horse, the one he always rode, was white. That day his aide was also mounted on a white horse. The aide was killed instead of Lafayette.

Nor did the king escape. Lafayette received information in Saint Antoine about that part of the plot in time to reach Versailles with his guards. There he disarmed the group of courtiers prepared to make off with Louis, Marie and their son.

The Vincennes incident handed Cordelier leaders fodder for propaganda: "Lafayette threatened to fire on the people" was the inciting news they bruited about. The disarming of the courtiers increased the bitterness of the royalists' hatred for him. Assessing his own situation at this time, he wrote to a friend abroad, the Marquis de Bouillé:

Paris has been divided into factions and the kingdom torn by anarchy. The violent aristocrats dream of a counter-revolution . . . On the left side you have . . . a club of

Jacobins which intends well, but the directors of which are everywhere causing disorders. . . . I am violently attacked by all party leaders who consider me an obstacle which it is impossible to corrupt or intimidate, and the first clause of every evil project is to overthrow me. . . . Add to this the double hatred, justly incurred . . . of the Orléanist party . . . add again the anger of Lameth, with whom I used to be intimately connected . . . as well as the dissatisfaction I give to those whom I prevent from pillaging Paris, and you will have the sum of what is working against me.

One might be tempted to call such a report paranoid, had a lesser man than Lafayette written it. Coming from him, the description was simply a realistic accounting of problems that had to be handled. On Easter day, 1791, an incident occurred which made him doubt that he could continue to stay on top of them. The Easter communion of the royal family was traditionally made at the cathedral of Notre Dame in Paris, but the clergy there that year had all taken the loyalty oath to the State and the king preferred to receive the bread and wine from a nonjuring priest. Accordingly, he decided to attend a church in the suburb of St. Cloud, whose priest had refused to conform.

Lafayette, acquainted with the king's desire, brought a company of guards to the Tuileries to protect the king's passage. By then rumors of the king's hope of an escape were rife, and Lafayette was well aware that the royal family's departure in their coach for church could be mistaken for an escape effort. If not so interpreted, it could still antagonize the many supporters of the new church law. Lafayette was one of those advocates, but he also believed deeply in freedom of religion for every man, for the king as for others. He felt Louis had a right to worship where he pleased.

Georges Jacques Danton did not. Danton was a leader of the Cordeliers, also an official of the Paris Commune and a member of the Assembly. An advocate of terrorism as the most serviceable weapon of revolution, and ambitious to be in charge of the terror, he viewed Lafayette's moderate policies as an infuriating stumbling block in the way of his goal. On Easter Sunday he collected a crowd of Cordelier sympathizers and of the rapidly growing radical wing of the Jacobins. The crowd surrounded the royal carriage, refusing to let it pass. Lafayette ordered the guards to disperse the crowd.

They refused.

The soldiers had been thoroughly propagandized by Orléanists and a Cordelier-Jacobin team. As quickly as possible, Lafayette brought up another battalion, but by then the king had ordered his coach to return to the palace. Lafayette followed him to urge that he make another try.

The king refused.

Lafayette felt certain that law would have been upheld by the crack battalion he had mustered. The king's refusal to proceed permitted the mob to register a victory against the law as represented in the person of the king.

Lafayette went straight to the Commune. There he presented his resignation. The guard had disobeyed orders, the symbol of the law was a spineless coward. Under those circumstances he could see no useful role for himself. He was so shaken that on reaching City Hall, he fainted. Some officials revived him; they pleaded with him to retain his command. They well knew that Lafayette stood not only between mob rule and the king's rule—nominal as that was now—but also between the mob and the Commune. The people were as capable of turning on the Commune as on the king. Without Lafayette Paris would be in an uproar, the officials said. But their arguments were of no avail. Lafayette remained firm in his resolve to withdraw.

Some of the members of the Commune went to talk with members of the National Guard. The guard, too, had reason to fear a mob out of hand. The following day representative guardsmen apologized to Lafayette for their lack of discipline. They pledged unquestioning obedience from then on. At that point Lafayette relented. Paris relaxed.

But not for long. On the night of June 20th, the royal family did flee. Emigrés were waiting for them at the northeast border. In the morning Lafayette signed an order for the arrest of his king. As he did so, he could hear a gathering crowd outside his headquarters shouting "Lafayette, traitor to the people! Lafayette, traitor!" The key instigator of the mob was Danton, who had spread word that Lafayette had deliberately permitted the escape. From Lafayette's quarters, the mob marched to the Tuileries, from which they were driven out by guardsmen acting on Lafayette's orders. Roused by the action of the guard, popular fear of a counterrevolution surfaced, and, skillfully manipulated by Danton, focused on Lafayette. To make matters worse, Lafayette was not as blameless in the situation as he had been on previous occasions where he had been the object of public wrath. Guard Commander, he was responsible for keeping the king at the Tuileries. There was no question but that he had failed in this responsibility, even though the failure had not been, as charged, deliberate.

It was Lafayette's comrade of the American Revolution, Alexandre Lameth, and others of the more levelheaded Jacobins who, two days later, came to his rescue. News reached the Assembly of trouble in a Jacobin club meeting. It had been invaded by Danton and others, who were calling for Lafayette's arrest. Jacobin Assemblymen hastened to the meeting. Lameth took Lafayette with him and two men entered arm in arm.

As they did so Danton shouted, "Monsieur le Commandant Général has promised on his head that the king would not go. We demand either the person of the king or the head of the Commandant Général!" Five hundred members of the club roared approval. Lameth quieted them.

"Once," he revealed, "Danton came to see me and asked whether it was necessary to ruin Lafayette. Is it not so, Monsieur?" Danton admitted that was the truth. "And is it not true," Lameth continued, "that I answered he had done much for liberty, and if liberty is threatened, you will see us reunited?" He added, "If the constitution were threatened, Monsieur Lafayette would die for it." Lameth's words sobered the audience. Lafayette was given a chance to explain his position. Conscious that he had been deceived by Louis and ought to have been wiser, he spoke with embarrassment, stammering and repeating himself. But he didn't try to deny his responsibility. He promised the king's arrest within forty-eight hours.

The king and queen were apprehended and brought back to Paris within the time limit. Lafayette met them at the Pantin gate where they entered, and followed their coach to the Tuileries. National Guardsmen lined the route, holding back the crowd. The people were silent, almost as though stunned. Not till the carriage reached the Tuileries, did their anger burst. Then, breaking through a line of guards, a group attempted to seize the foreign bodyguards who had accompanied the royal family in flight. The queen shouted to Lafayette to save their lives. Lafayette and two officers broke up the assault. There was no further difficulty.

Inside the palace, the king had the grace to thank Lafayette for the escort. Lafayette's reply was a warning. "Your Majesty knows my attachment to the monarch as an institution, but I have never disguised the fact that the moment Your Majesty separates his cause from the cause of the people, I remain with the people."

The queen, who, a few moments ago, had been crying to Lafayette for rescue, curled her lips as he spoke. She held out her jewel box to him. "This will save you the trouble of rifling it," she said. Lafayette turned away. The queen shrugged. "No doubt I shall meet others with less pretense," she remarked.

As the family entered their bedrooms, Lafayette posted sentinels at their doors. The people's prisoners would not escape again.

For a little more than three weeks an uneasy peace reigned in Paris. With the aid of Orléans and his followers, the Cordeliers doubled their efforts to upset it. They were busy with a petition which declared that the king's flight should be interpreted as giving up the throne. They demanded a vote of the nation to determine whether or not he should be reinstated. The petition was ruled illegal by the Assembly President as "an attack on the Constitution." Nevertheless, the Cordeliers were determined to have it read in public.

On July 16th, they took it to the Champ de Mars, a Paris parade ground that stretched from the national military training school to the River Seine. Between reviews of the military, the people used it as a park. At one end an altar of the revolution had been erected, known as the National Altar. From this altar, Danton proposed to read the petition. As he mounted, a small crowd of the curious gathered. When he finished reading they dispersed, having shown little interest.

The following day being a Sunday, a larger crowd might be expected if the day was fine. It dawned hot and sultry. The parade grounds filled rapidly with strollers. A story buzzed from group to group that two guards were hiding under the altar, prepared to blow to bits any petitioners who attempted to read the document a second time. There were indeed two men under the altar, but they weren't guards. They were harmless vagabonds who had been enjoying a night's free shelter. Despite their astounded protests, they were slaughtered. Lafayette was sent for.

When he arrived, someone fired at him, point blank. This was the second attempt on his life in five months. Fortunately, it, too, failed. The pistol misfired. National Guards seized the would-be assassin, but Lafayette refused to have him arrested. Whereupon some Jacobins circulated the story the drama had been staged. The crowd didn't seem to care. On the river bank, a fiddler began to play. People drifted toward him, dancers choosing partners.

Lafayette remained on the field. With him was the Mayor of Paris, Jean Bailly. By noon the heat had become oppressive. The dancers wilted. A group gathered around the petitioners who had just arrived. Their original petition having been ruled illegal, they had decided to write a new one. They sat down in front of the altar to compose it. The gist of their request was that a convention be organized to try the king.

Not far from the writers, Lafayette and Bailly were talking. "There is a storm about, don't you feel it?" Lafayette asked. Bailly took the question to refer to the people's mood. "We must be ready for any emergency," he replied. "I have the red flag with me." The red flag was the signal to declare martial law.

The crowd had begun to mill. Some started throwing stones. They selected Lafayette's aide-de-camp as a target. Guards stepped in and the stoning stopped. By late afternoon, the crowd had doubled in size; disputes arose among various club factions; bricks, stones and bottles were hurled. Cordons of armed civilians appeared. Up went the red flag.

The guards moved in to disperse the mob. They were hissed and cursed. They rolled their drums in warning and fired into the air. But the crowds did not back off. Exasperated, unaccustomed to such resistance, and irritated at being called up for duty on a Sunday, the guards, without waiting for orders, fired directly into the mob. That did it. The people rushed off in terror. On the field, in the gathering dusk, fifteen lay dead.

Within forty-eight hours, half Paris was convinced that five hundred peaceful citizens had been murdered, their bodies thrown into the Seine. Lafayette, friend of the people, was called tyrant by the people he had befriended. Traitor and tyrant. The author of the Declaration of Rights had already begun to learn that the capacity for self-discipline with which he had once hopefully clad his image of the common man couldn't always be counted on. In fact he was finding it was often most apt to fail when most needed. Ruefully, he conceded that on the Champ de Mars, the guards and the people had been equally undisciplined.

True, Paris had quieted down again afterward. Danton had been temporarily forced to flee, the Cordeliers' club was outlawed. But these had been emergency measures, not the outgrowth of the people's reasoned will. True, an elected Assembly ruled the nation, but without the strength of Lafayette's National Guard, that rule would not survive. Lafayette knew himself to be, in effect, a military dictator. A hero for fifteen years, he was now well hated. Yet Paris depended upon him for the maintenance of order. The people didn't really want to tear themselves apart. This Lafayette also knew. Thus, when friends begged him not to walk the streets alone, he replied, "I have never been in greater safety, since the streets are filled with people."

On September 4th, the Assembly finished the work of writing a constitution. It would soon break up in favor of a new lawmaking body—a legislative assembly. The king, presiding at the final session, accepted the first Constitution of France. "Sire," said the President, "in accepting, you have ended the revolution." "Let the nation resume its happy nature," the king replied.

A great celebration was held on the Champ-de-Mars, with Lafayette riding his white horse at the head of his guards. The Assembly presented him with a sword forged from melted-down locks of the Bastille. On the surface, the memory of the blood so recently shed on the parade ground seemed erased. The Jacobins had split into two factions; the majority had gone over to the Feuillants. Moderation appeared once again to have triumphed.

But behind the scenes a different drama was being acted

out. The remaining hard-core Jacobins referred to the Feuil-lants as *Feuilles Mortes*—dead leaves. Lafayette was the "general of the dead leaves." "Counterrevolutionaries" the extremists called them, circulating cartoons that showed them hobbling about on canes, like old men. Biding their time, these revolutionaries of the future watched what the equally hard-core royalists were presently about. Marie Antoinette was plotting with the core. War threatened. Meanwhile, the harvest was a quarter of what it had been the year before; there would soon be discontent among the people—all grist to the radicals' mill. Let the nation resume its happy nature?

# 5

## *Patriot in Prison*

W ITH the passage of the Constitution, Lafayette felt that all he could do for the time being, he had done. A republic had been established; its law spelled out. To enforce this new order would be the job of new civil authorities. He was not, however, among the many who, standing at this turning point, had no doubts about the future. The events of the last two years had gradually flattened the sparkling optimism with which, in his letter to George Washington, he had hailed the gathering of the Notables as a beginning that "would lead to great good."

The tone of the letter he wrote Washington in mid-September of 1791, informing him of Louis's acceptance of the Constitution, was far more guarded.

The document is a long way from perfection. I especially regret that we who see the advantages of a two part legislature were unable to prevail on a sufficient majority to incorporate that feature. But allowance is made for amendment, and as weaknesses become apparent, one hopes strength will come with changes. I pray that the changes may take place peacefully: already there has been too much of force. But the moods of the people are capricious and there are ambitious men who do not scruple to play upon these for their personal advancement.

We suffer much from the death of Mirabeau last April. He and I were not friendly and I fear he was not above accepting rewards from the court for his pursuit of moderation, but however that may be, he was, by conviction, a constitutional monarchist and both by his oratory and his parliamentary skill, he was able to carry along many with his stand.

A fortnight after this report to Washington, *Mr.* Lafayette —the Assembly had abolished all titles—went home to Chavaniac. Paris had stood in awe of him because his presence was a guarantee of public order; the reverence with which he was greeted in Auvergne was personal. The Avergnats saluted the man he had become, the service he had given Frenchmen.

He had been home only a few days when dignitaries from nearby towns and villages, Brioude, Puy, Yssingeaux and Monistrol, called at Chavaniac to express their gratitude. Each delegation brought an invitation to a civic celebration in his honor. Lafayette accepted them all.

With him on these occasions were Adrienne, his three children, Georges Washington, Virginie and Anastasie, also Adrienne's aunt and grandmother. The latter pair had for some time been occupying Chavaniac. They were meticulous tenants. The Lafayettes came home to a prosperous chateau gleaming with black marble fireplaces, gilt framed mirrors and mahogany ceiling beams. Outside, hedges were clipped and flower gardens manicured.

Terraced hillside vineyards had yielded the grapes for the Saint-Pourçain and Châteaugay wine which stocked Chavaniac's cellar. Lafayette tasted to approve the vintage, but drank only sparingly. His distaste for alcohol grew stronger as he grew older. Prudence, his natural inclination in personal life, had reined the youthful efforts he had once made to imitate his peers and in particular his hard-drinking brother-in-law, Paul de Noailles.

His looks, too, had changed with the passage of time. His formerly bland facial expression had given way to one of solemnity. The doll-like Cupid's bow lips had straightened out, wiping from his face the impression of a painted smile. Below his eyes, flesh was beginning to fold and the recessed chin was beginning to double. Above his high forehead, his hair had started to recede.

At thirty-four, he had, in fact, an air of weariness. He needed the restoration that Chavaniac always gave when his spirits sagged; he needed the rugged quietude of the mountains as well as the warm welcome of his fellow Auvergnats. To a friend in Paris, Madame de Simiane, he wrote:

> My neighbors have proffered me all imaginable festivities. The genuineness of their welcome touches me deeply. . . . I have found Chavaniac in excellent condition, thanks to Mmes. d'Ayen and de Noailles. Just now, as I write, my pear orchard is being harvested. It is red with the color of autumn and so are the vineyards on the slopes beyond. Mme. de Lafayette joins me in the hope that you will pay us a visit soon. We cannot offer you the excitement of all the events in Paris, but we can offer you a very soothing peace.

That peace was short-lived, as all his adult interludes at Chavaniac seemed to be. In early December he was ordered to Metz to command a fifty-two-thousand-man army, one of three such being prepared for war with Austria and the emigrés. With him was his old friend from American Revolutionary days, Rochambeau. He found the army in bad shape, mentally and militarily. A third of the officers had deserted to the emigrés. The soldiers were poorly clothed, badly armed. With his particular skill for rallying troops, he re-equipped his men and remodeled them into some semblance of a fighting force.

In April, France formally declared war on Austria. Lafayette was once again on the battlefield. Prussia joined Austria and the fighting did not go well for the French on any of the fronts where armies had been deployed. Fear of defeat, of an invasion which would restore monarchy, shook the Assembly in Paris and the people throughout the nation. A kind of hysteria took over. Jacobin clubs promoted riots. No street was safe for ordinary citizens. Terrorists roamed at will, threatening lives and looting property. On the political level, Jacobin strength was such that they were able to select and install one of their own as Minister of War and another as Mayor of Paris. They were approaching their goal of taking over the Assembly.

When news of this state of affairs reached Lafayette, he immediately wrote a letter to the Assembly, denouncing Jacobin conduct. "Unconstitutional," he said. When the Assembly President read the letter aloud, the session turned into an uproar, with the Jacobins countercharging that Lafayette was preparing to aid Prussia and Austria in the conquest of France. Shortly afterwards, a Jacobin mob, angered by the king's refusal to pass two measures signed by the Assembly, crashed into the Tuileries, raided its cellar, and guzzling bottles of wine, invaded the royal chambers. The leaders forced the king to drink with them, placing on his head a revolutionary stocking cap. Into Marie Antoinette's face they blew the smoke from their cigarettes.

As soon as Lafayette heard of this incident, he determined to return to Paris. General Luckner, who was commanding the French army along the Rhine River, urged him not to go. "They will have your head," he warned. But Lafayette was not to be shaken. In a letter replying to Luckner, he explained:

> Since I have breathed, it has been only for the cause of liberty. I can no longer submit in silence to the tyranny exercised by factions over the National Assembly and the

king, in obliging the former to swerve from the constitution which we have all sworn to defend, and in putting the latter in imminent danger both as to his political and physical existence.

This is my profession of faith and it is that of nineteen out of twenty throughout the kingdom, but they are afraid. For my part, who am a stranger to that malady I shall speak the truth.

Speak it he did. On June 28th, he strode into the Assembly session to repeat his charge of unconstitutionality against the Jacobins. When the Assembly supported the charge, he urged the members to outlaw the Jacobin clubs. Only thirteen delegates were ready to take such extreme action. They feared revenge. As for the Jacobins, they labeled Lafayette a "rascal, traitor and enemy of the people." From that moment on, they looked for a chance to do away with him unless, as some counseled, "the rascal can be used on our side."

From the Assembly, Lafayette hastened to the Tuileries. There, having gathered a contingent of tried and trusted National Guards, he placed them at the gates to defend the royal family, in case of another invasion. For his pains he received a cold shoulder from the court and the queen. "Better to perish," said she, "than to be saved by Monsieur de Lafayette and the Constitutionals."

Having done all he could, he returned to the front. But his all was not enough. No one man's finger in the dike—not even Lafayette's—could hold back the rising tide of hysteria. The moderates lacked the guts for action; the royalists clung stubbornly to their position. Between them they were opening the floodgates of the nation for the Reign of Terror.

The major rulers in that reign were Marat, Danton and Maximilien Robespierre, a Jacobin leader, Assembly and Paris Commune member who was convinced that the Revolution could succeed only by tough dictatorial means. The major troops they commanded were the Jacobins, the "Mountain" in the Assembly and a wildcat Commune which took over the government of Paris. Later their ranks were swelled by members of the Committee of Public Safety and the Revolutionary Tribunal Council, two extremist groups created by the Assembly at the insistence of the "Mountain."

Told of the worsening situation, Lafayette wanted to march his troops to Paris in support of the king and against the Jacobins. The king, at the queen's urging, rejected the plan. Not he, but she replied to Lafayette's messengers, saying, "It would be better for us to be shut up . . . in a tower." She needn't have wasted her breath. Lafayette's soldiers refused to budge. The Jacobins had been busy among them. The soldiers even refused to swear loyalty to the constitution.

The Jacobins' next move was to introduce in the Assembly a resolution to impeach Lafayette. Based on statements in his letter to Luckner, of which they had obtained a copy, they declared:

The National Assembly, considering that Mr. Lafayette . . . by taking an active part in the administration of civil and political affairs of the empire . . . has openly violated the constitutional law which forbids the armed forces to deliberate; that he has therein endeavored to debase the National Assembly, in supposing it governed by a faction; that he has slandered the acts of the Assembly in saying that they deviate from the constitution;—considering that the legislative power cannot, without a criminal weakness, and without emboldening transgressors . . . tolerate . . . proceedings which so directly mitigate against the national representation and the laws of the land;—decree that there is sufficient ground of impeachment against Mr. Lafayette.

But not quite yet could the Jacobins pull all the strings of the Assembly. With six hundred and thirty members present, the resolution was turned down by a vote of four hundred and six to two hundred and twenty-four. Furious, the Jacobins gathered a new mob to march again on the Tuileries. In it, Parisians mingled with citizens who had marched from Marseilles to join the protest against monarchy. The men of Marseilles were singing a song just composed by Rouget de Lisle, a musically-minded soldier in Luckner's army. He had intended the tune to spur on the French defenders of the Rhine, but the words and music fitted perfectly the mood of the marchers.

> Rise up, offspring of the fatherland, the day of glory has come! Against us, the bloody banner of tyranny has been lifted on high! To arms citizens! Form your batallions!
> March, march on, let (their) polluted blood soak our fields!
> Sacred love of country, direct, support our avenging arms! Liberty, dear liberty, combat your expiring enemies. Behold your triumph and our glory. To arms, citizens, etc.

Paradoxically, de Lisle was a royalist. His song, soon known as the "Marseillaise," because of its Paris introduction by men of Marseilles, became the rally chant of the revolution and subsequently, the French National Anthem.

The first group of Parisians to sing it meant business. Bloody business. For them no guzzling of wine from the palace cellar. Methodically, they murdered the Tuileries guards, including those posted by Lafayette, mounted their heads on spikes, captured the royal family and imprisoned all three in the tower of a Paris fortress. The jailing of king, queen and dauphin was followed by the jailing of some three thousand nobles, nonjuring priests and others accused of sympathizing with the Austrians and the emigrés. Hundreds of these prisoners were executed with the barest pretense of a trial. The purpose, in the minds of Marat and the Paris Commune who directed the massacre, was to frighten

# Marseillaise

1. Al - lons, en - fants de la pa - tri — e, Le jour de
2. A - mour sa - cré de la pa - tri — e, Con - duis, sou -

gloire est ar - ri - vé; Con - tre
tiens nos bras ven - geurs! Li - ber -

nous de la ty - ran - ni - e, L'é - ten -
té, Li - ber-té ché — ri - e, Com - bats

dard sang - lant est le - vé. L'é - ten -
a - vec tes dé - fen - seurs, Com - bats

dard sang - lant est le - vé. En - ten - dez
a - vec tes dé - fen - seurs. Sous nos dra -

vous dans nos cam - pag - nes Mu -
peaux que la vic - toi - re Ac -

gir ces fé - ro - ces sol - dats? Ils
coure à tes mâ - les ac - cents! Que

vien - nent jus-que dans nos bras É - gor - ger nos fils, nos com -
tes en - ne-mis ex - pi - rants Voient ton tri-omphe et — no - tre

pa - gnes. Aux ar — mes, ci - toy - ens! For -
gloi - re.

mez — vos ba-tail - lons! Mar - chons, mar - chons!

Qu'un sang im - pur A - breu — ve nos sil - lons.

into submission any who still harbored hope of return to an absolute monarchy, or even held out for constitutional monarchy.

The horrified Lafayette was helpless at Metz. On September 17th, the executive council of the Jacobins ordered him to turn over his command to one of their men and return immediately to Paris. They had previously offered him the presidency of the republic if he would agree to abandon the king and the Constitution. They were aware that his influence would enhance their plans. Lafayette had, of course, refused. He correctly interpreted the summons to Paris which followed his refusal as a death warrant. He decided to seek asylum in the United States.

He never made it. The Assembly, now completely controlled by the Jacobins, issued an order for his arrest. "Mr. Lafayette" was "wanted for rebellion against the law, for conspiracy against liberty, for plotting against the nation." On Sunday morning, August 19th, he set out with a group of loyal officers and orderlies, among them Alexandre Lameth, hoping to reach Holland. En route, the little party was captured by the Austrians. Some were allowed to go. Some were given mild imprisonment in Antwerp, Belgium. But Lafayette, Alexandre Lameth and other "name" revolutionary leaders were clapped into a dungeon in Wesel, Prussia, as "prisoners of the state." There was no need for trial under the code of law of their captors. A prisoner of state was assumed guilty. "The existence of Lafayette as a free man is incompatible with the safety of the governments of Europe," the king of Prussia declared.

The Wesel prison was the first of three in which Lafayette was to spend the next five years. Lightless, rat-infested and cold, the dungeon, from which prisoners were not even allowed out for exercise, offered living death. Better surroundings would be available, the King of Prussia advised, if Lafayette would provide information which Austria and Prussia could use to defeat France. Lafayette refused. He was at this point so ill with fever that his captors feared he would die. This they did not want, at least, not then. Though in due time they might consider hanging him, he could in the meanwhile prove valuable as a hostage. Nor was this the time to make him a martyr. Such action might even provoke some of his enemies.

So, at the end of a year in Wesel, he was transferred to Magdeburg. There conditions were somewhat better. By bribing a guard, he was able to obtain charcoal, a toothpick and an occasional sheet of paper. With these he could write letters. He also was permitted to receive mail. His friends, who had despaired of ever seeing him again, began to hear from him. On the way to Wesel, he had been able to get in touch with the American Minister to Holland, asking that he be claimed as an American citizen, and to write advising his wife of his plight, suggesting that she go to England and join him later in the States. But after this one contact, the American Minister could find no further trace of Lafayette. No one was talking. The Minister wrote to Gouverneur Morris, then U.S. Minister to France, "It is certain that he (Lafayette) is the man whom the Austrians and Prussians hate most . . . They wish no doubt to smother the affair and the victims also."

The first indication of Lafayette's whereabouts came in a letter he wrote to the Princess d'Henin in Paris, on May 15, 1793, describing his cell at Magdeburg:

Imagine a hollow in the ramparts of the citadel, protected by a high and strong palisade. From there four successive doors, each secured by chains, padlocks and iron bars open into my dungeon, three feet wide by five and a half feet long. It is lugubrious, damp, and offers me for decoration two French verses which rhyme with *souffrir* [to suffer] and *mourir* [to die]. The wall on the moat side is moldy

and the other one lets daylight, but no sunlight, penetrate
by a small grilled window . . .

My health deteriorates daily; my physical constitution has
almost as much need of liberty, as my moral constitution.
The lack of air in this subterranean cell is destroying my
chest. I have often fever, no exercise and little sleep, but I
insist on staying alive . . .

His health became so fragile that his captors called in a
physician, who insisted on exercise and fresh air. Thereafter,
Lafayette was permitted to walk on the ramparts for a short
period daily. The walks also gave him opportunity to con-
verse with Lameth and others who were his fellow prisoners.

In the meanwhile, Washington and Jefferson, who had
become United States Secretary of State, had not been idle in
his behalf, even though they were for a year unable to locate
him. His request to be claimed as an American citizen they
did not feel they could grant without straining to the breaking point their young republic's relationship with European
countries. However, they did everything short of making
such a claim. Washington requested Jefferson to draft for his
signature a letter to all American ministers in Europe, asking
them to express informally to monarchs of the countries
where they were assigned the concern of the United States
for the fate of Lafayette.

Jefferson's draft went much further than Washington had
suggested, but Washington signed it without changing a
word. "If formal solicitations be necessary," read the Jefferson draft, "you are authorized to signify . . . that our government and nation, faithful in their attachment to this gentleman for the services he has rendered them, feel a lively
interest in his welfare, and will view his liberation as a mark
of consideration and friendship for the United States, and a
new motive for esteem and reciprocation of kind offices
towards the power to whom they shall be indebted for this

act." Washington had specified an informal expression of American sentiments: Jefferson made it "formal if necessary."

Gouverneur Morris saw to it that funds were made available to Adrienne, as well as placing funds in an Amsterdam bank for Lafayette's use in the event of his release. Washington placed funds to Adrienne's credit in the same bank and to save her embarrassment wrote, "This sum is, I am certain, the least I am indebted for services rendered to me by the Marquis de Lafayette."

Adrienne, on receiving her husband's letter the previous year, had attempted to follow his advice and escape to England. She sent her son, Georges Washington, with his tutor, Frestel, to a hiding place offered by a priest in the mountains of Auvergne, buried Lafayette's papers and was on her way with the two daughters when she was arrested. She was not jailed, however—merely placed on parole at Chavaniac. This clemency lasted about a year, during which she devoted herself to the girls' education, while Frestel continued to teach Georges.

In the late fall of 1793, Adrienne was thrown into jail in Brioude, and her mother, grandmother and sister imprisoned in Luxembourg. Daughters Anastasie and Virginie were spared. Frestel arranged for them to visit their mother occasionally, traveling by night and hiding by day. Subsequently she was transferred to a Paris prison. Anastasie attempted to accompany her, but was prevented by the revolutionary authorities in Brioude.

Adrienne remained a captive until January, 1795, when James Monroe, American Minister to France, backed up by the former Minister, Gouverneur Morris, succeeded in obtaining her release. Morris had written the French Commissioner of Exterior Relations that the death of Lafayette's wife would seriously antagonize American public opinion. Monroe followed up on this letter. Otherwise Adrienne, too, would doubtless have suffered the fate of her mother, sister and grandmother. They were guillotined.

During Adrienne's years in prison, the Reign of Terror reached its heights. The giant-bladed guillotine had been invented as a means of beheading more people in less time, but the list of victims mounted with such frenzy that jails were bursting with the condemned. The pretexts were often slight. Whole families could be sentenced because one relative was an emigré or had made some statement considered counterrevolutionary.

The monarchy was abolished, the king, queen, and dauphin executed. So was the double-dealing Duke d'Orléans, who had joined the Mountain and voted for the death of the king. Much good it did him. A few months after he joined, his son deserted to the Austrians. Hence the guillotine for the father. With the end of the monarchy, a new constitution had to be written; a convention was called for that purpose. The Assembly dissolved itself in favor of the convention.

Left without administrative machinery, France was ruled by the Committee of Public Safety, appointed from among Assembly members, and by the similarly appointed Revolutionary Tribunal Council. The majority of the Girondists, still clinging to a philosophy of moderation, were arrested, many of them guillotined. Finally Danton, now head of the Committee of Public Safety, had had enough. He switched to the dwindling forces of the moderates. Robespierre, his rival on the Committee, had him guillotined, likewise Camille Desmoulins, who had also switched. Conveniently for Robespierre, Marat was stabbed. Robespierre ruled, dictator of all France.

Some of the news of the anarchy, and bloodshed in which the ideals of the original revolutionists were foundering, filtered or was smuggled into Magdeburg. Brooding over it, Lafayette wrote to a Paris friend of "inexpressible grief . . . at finding myself after sixteen years of labor compelled to deny myself the happiness of combatting for the principles, the sentiments, and the purposes for which I have always lived." In his mind, he began to go over and over the events leading up to his imprisonment. Had he brought upon himself this exile from the scene of action? Could he have behaved otherwise? No, he could not. "I am far from repenting my combat, I would do the same thing again, even if it ended in the same results."

The months at Magdeburg were months of deep reflection. The hardships damaged his health, but the isolation nourished his mind. He began to think not only personally, but historically, to analyze the revolution. What had gone wrong with it? His answer was: the rapid elimination of the monarchy:

> The meaning of the word republic is a pure popular government without any mixture of monarch or aristocracy. Such was the mode designed to produce liberty, and consequently the happiness of mankind. But wanting the due and necessary ingredients, it has failed and ever will fail in producing the end proposed. The goodness of the intention admitted, the means are imperfect. . . . On the other hand it has been amply proved that a happy mixture of monarchy . . . will make the means perfectly equal to the original design . . . Monarchy unites an infinite number of parts and gives them one . . . firm . . . and inseparable body.

Yet, in the face of the revolution's failure and his own fate, he resolutely continued to believe in the future. "Liberty, in the midst of the violence of anarchy and so many hostile attacks, will not perish, in spite of its enemies." His passion, his mistress, would survive.

The time for reflection and writing was short-lived. In less than a year he was transferred to a prison at Olmütz, near the Polish border. There he was permitted no mail, could procure no writing implements. Books, which he had been al-

The States-General meets on May 5, 1789 for the first time in 176 years. *Courtesy of the French Embassy Press and Information Division.*

The Declaration of the Rights of Man and the Citizen. *Courtesy of the French Embassy Press and Information Division.*

The Third Estate, meeting in the *Jeu de Paume,* takes an oath to stay together. *Courtesy of the French Embassy Press and Information Division.*

The Storming of the Bastille. *Courtesy of the French Embassy Press and Information Division.*

Nobles in the National Assembly rise to give up the privileges of birth, August 4, 1789. *Courtesy of the French Embassy Press and Information Division.*

Lafayette presents the tricolor cockade he
conceived to the Commune of Paris. *Courtesy
of the Lafayette Memorial Foundation.*

Lafayette in front of City Hall on the way to present his
resignation as National Guard Commander to the Commune
of Paris, Easter Sunday, 1791. *Courtesy of the French Embassy
Press and Information Division.*

lowed at will in Magdeburg, were carefully scrutinized. He was not allowed any which contained the word "liberty." The guards could not be bribed for favors; they simply helped themselves to what little of value he still possessed and might have bargained with—his knee and collar buckles, his watch, even his razor.

His meals were served in bowls which were only very occasionally washed. He was given no knife, fork or spoon. When he asked for them he was told it was feared he might commit suicide with them. "Messieurs," he replied, "I am not obliging enough to do that." However, no cutlery came, so he ate with his fingers. When a guard asked if this manner of dining wasn't strange to him, he answered, "Not at all. I have employed it in America when eating with Indians." Dirty, sick, bearded, ragged, he remained the republican aristocrat—faithful to his convictions, contained in attitude, handling adversity with flashes of wit which were a new leaven in his personality.

The cell at Olmütz was narrower and darker than any he had been in. The town sewage flowed in open gutters past his dungeon, and the rank stench drifted through an aperture high above Lafayette's head. So did swarms of mosquitoes. But two advantages there were. When Lafayette began to have violent coughing spells, the authorities feared he might suffocate. They permitted him well-guarded excursions by carriage into the countryside to get fresh air. They also sent a physician, a Dr. Haberlein, to attend to him. Haberlein had a profound admiration for George Washington. When he could be sure that guards weren't eavesdropping at the cell door, he questioned Lafayette about the American Revolution and the two men had long, stimulating conversations about the philosophy of the men who fought it.

As the talks progressed, the doctor's relationship with Lafayette grew far beyond the professional. He began to feel a moral obligation to preserve not only his patient's body, but also his patient's spirit. He made contact with a German student by the name of Justus Erich Bollman, who had long been an admirer of Lafayette and was seeking his whereabouts. He told Lafayette of the contact and supplied him with a quill, paper and lemon juice so that he could busy himself by corresponding with Bollman. Haberlein carried the correspondence back and forth. The lemon juice substitute for ink was legible only when held against fire, a necessary precaution, since Haberlein's medical kit and pockets were subject to inspection on entry and exit from the prison.

Bollman, meanwhile, had met in a Vienna coffee house Francis Huger, the son of the Major Benjamin Huger who had welcomed Lafayette to Charleston on his first visit to the United States. Francis had journeyed to Vienna to study surgery. Together, the two young men began to plot for Lafayette's escape.

Through Haberlein they communicated to Lafayette that the attempt to free him was to be made on the eighth of November, during a carriage excursion scheduled for that date. Two horsemen would pass his carriage, pausing as they did so. By the pause, Lafayette would know they were his rescuers. He, in turn, was to pass his hand across his forehead, so that they could be sure of recognizing him. Lafayette and Bollman had never met and Huger's boyhood memory of the Marquis his father had entertained seventeen years ago was too dim and distant to be serviceable. They had only a picture to guide them.

The recognition process went perfectly. After the horsemen passed, pausing, Lafayette suggested to one of the two guards accompanying him that they stop at a nearby tavern for a drink, to which the guard readily agreed. As soon as they stepped down from the carriage, Lafayette tackled one guard and Huger, who had returned with Bollman from a short way down the road, tackled the other. Bollman went for the driver.

Lafayette managed to knock out the guard he struggled

with, though at the price of a sprained back and a hand bitten nearly through. Bollman tied up the driver. Huger's opponent escaped and ran off to seek help. Huger handed Lafayette a pair of pistols and the reins of his horse. "Get to Hoff," he said. Hoff was a village where Huger and Bollman had arranged for documents, disguise, a carriage—all that Lafayette would need to reach Holland.

Lafayette misunderstood Huger. He thought he said, "Get off." He "got off" to the nearest town, Sternberg, where he was arrested. Bollman and Huger were captured and imprisoned for eight months. Lafayette was returned to Olmütz. Looking back on his reentry to the Olmütz dungeon, he wrote in his memoirs, "I had nothing left to do but defend my own constitution constantly, and apparently with as little success as I defended the national Constitution."

In the meanwhile Adrienne had been released from prison. She told Charles Fox, a former foreign minister of England who sympathized with the moderate French revolutionists, that she had but one desire: "to travel on the wings of duty and love in order to share my husband's captivity." She would take her daughters with her.

First, however, she had to arrange for the safety of Georges. She intended to send him to George Washington in America. When her plan for his escape fell through, she appealed to James Monroe for help. Monroe obtained an American passport for Georges in the name of Motier, to which he was entitled, his father being an honorary citizen of several American states. However, Georges also needed a French travel document. The Viscount de Ségur then introduced Adrienne to a moderate member of the Committee of Public Safety, Boissy d'Anglas, whose political views were similar to Lafayette's. D'Anglas agreed to get the signatures of his colleagues on the travel document without revealing Georges' identity. But, he said, the request for the document would have to be submitted by an American.

At this juncture, Monroe persuaded a Boston merchant,

Thomas Handasyd Perkins, to make the request. It was granted and Perkins and another merchant, Joseph Russell, put up the money for Georges' passage aboard the *Betsey,* a ship in which Perkins had an interest. He supplied Georges with a letter for the ship's captain, Thomas Sturgis. All went well and the ship sailed from Le Havre. Frestel took passage on a separate vessel later.

In Boston Georges stayed with Russell's father, Joseph, Sr., then town treasurer. He was also watched over by Mrs. Perkins, her brother, Simon Elliott, and the Perkins brothers, James and Samuel, all of whom lived nearby. The knowledge of his identity was known to this small circle alone.

In late August, Frestel having arrived, the two called on a revolutionary comrade of Lafayette's, General Knox, who was a retired Secretary of War. The old soldier took an immediate fancy to Georges and wrote to Washington asking him to receive the young man. He probably also enclosed the letter for Washington which Adrienne had given her son. "My wish is," she wrote tactfully, "that my son . . . should resume his studies interrupted by three years of misfortunes, and that . . . he may become fit to fulfill the duties of a citizen of the United States whose feelings will always agree with those of a French citizen."

Knox's appeal put the President of the United States in a spot. His natural instinct was to take Georges in immediately. His political instinct warned against such action. The Revolutionary Government of France was at that moment at war with England and claimed that the United States was obliged by the treaties of 1778 through which France had become our ally, to support her side. War was the last thing the infant American union needed. Washington proclaimed neutrality. Further, he sent his Chief Justice of the Supreme Court, John Jay, to England to negotiate a treaty which narrowly kept us out of the conflict. The French were furious. Washington didn't want to add fuel to the fire.

So he compromised. He asked Senator George Cabot of Boston to call on Georges, assuring him that Washington would be his father and his friend, but at the same time pointing out why it would be unwise for him to come to the capital city at that time. Washington suggested that Georges enroll at Harvard University, and offered to pay the bill, but Frestel blocked the move.

Meanwhile the secret of Georges's presence in Boston was becoming known. Also life in the Russell household was becoming difficult. Mr. Russell had fallen ill, and his only daughter, who kept house for him, had died. With Senator Cabot's approval, Georges and Frestel moved to the home of a former aide-de-camp of Lafayette's, La Colombe, who was now a French exile living in Ramapo, New Jersey. With them they took a letter from Cabot to Alexander Hamilton, Washington's Secretary of the Treasury. Hamilton was to be the next to intervene with Washington.

Intervene he did, but still Washington agonized over what to do. Finally he wrote the French Ambassador who neither replied nor took any official notice of the situation. At that point Washington sent for Georges and installed him and Frestel at Mount Vernon. An architect named Latrobe, visiting Mount Vernon while Georges was there, recorded an impression of him: "Young Lafayette with his tutor came down sometime before dinner. He is a young man of about seventeen, of a mild pleasing countenance, favorably impressing at first sight. His manners are easy and he has very little of the French air about him. He talked much . . . and seemed to possess wit and fluency. He spoke English tolerably well, much better, indeed than his tutor."

While Georges had been living in America, his mother had fulfilled the desire she had confessed to Charles Fox. She journeyed to Vienna to call on the Austrian Emperor, Franz II. From him she obtained the permission she sought to join her husband in the Olmütz dungeon. On October 24, 1795, in a chill dawn, the carriage she had hired approached the walled, spired town. At the sight of the spires, Adrienne began reciting the canticle from the book of Tobit in the Apocrypha of the Bible, in which Tobit and his son Tobias praise God for their deliverance from a sea of troubles by an angel of the Lord:

> Thou art great O Lord forever, and Thy kingdom is unto all ages. For Thou scourgest and Thou savest; Thou leadest down to hell and bringest up again; and there is none that can escape Thy hand . . . My soul, bless thou the Lord . . . [Tobit: 13:2]

Lafayette had no idea that his wife and daughters were on their way to him. His memoirs give no account of what his emotions were when they stood framed in the doorway of his cell. He recorded only that the guards snatched Adrienne's purse, and after searching the family luggage removed the cutlery and writing materials. Later one senses his gratitude for their presence as he recalls how they improvised for his comfort. He tells for instance how daughter Virginie covered his bare feet with socks made from the sleeves of her sweater, while daughter Anastasie fashioned shoes from her mother's corset.

Anastasie, who had a sharp wit, used it to introduce some light moments into the grim prison existence. The guard, a brutish boor, wore his unkempt hair in a knot at the back of his head which, in eighteenth century France was called a *catogan*. Since he walked with the stealth associated with Iroquois Indians, Anastasie gave him the name *Cataquois*. Using a hairpin dipped in the juice of some cherries Haberlein had smuggled in, she drew on her thumbnail a caricature of Cataquois carrying his great keys and his club. The family couldn't help but laugh.

They all lived as Lafayette did. By day, mother and daughters occupied his cell. At night, Adrienne stayed with him; the two girls were given a separate sleeping cell. The four ate the prison slop together, with their fingers. Adrienne developed scurvy, but sickness was not what depressed her most; not attending Mass or being able to write her son were her greatest deprivations. Yet in a way she was happy. For the first time in her life, she had her husband to herself—all day and night, every day and night. She could—and did—lavish on him the pent-up love of twenty-two years. She ministered as best she could to his needs, and when his spirits lagged, rekindled them by holding up his basic conviction that some good for the welfare of mankind must issue from the Revolution despite its horrifying excesses.

The enormity of her sacrifice stunned him into an awareness of the depth of her devotion to him, and the intimacy of life in a tiny cell knit him physically and emotionally closer to her. There was no room at Olmütz for his customary aloofness. He became a husband to her. To the girls he had always been a preceptor. Now he became a father. The Lafayettes were finally a family. That was Adrienne's reward.

When Adrienne arrived, she brought news of the guillotining of Robespierre and the adoption of a new French Constitution—the third since the beginning of the Revolution. The new document gave executive power to a Directory of five men, legislative power to two chambers. Lafayette had always wanted a bicameral legislature, but he scoffed at the idea of the Directory. So did the people of France. The country was troubled with serious inflation as a result of the worthless revolutionary money, the assignats.

Meanwhile the Directory, whose personnel was not noted for brains, was living extremely well. They had easy access to a flourishing black market and they were happy with the dandified plumes, laces and silken breeches with which the legislature provided them. Less favored citizens called them "rotten bellies." To distract public attention from financial woes, the Directory started new wars. These brought to the fore an exceptional young soldier, who had already served with distinction in armies which were defeating Austria and Prussia. A few weeks before Adrienne's arrival at Olmütz, this twenty-six-year-old had become overnight the hero of Paris by dispersing a royalist mob on the warpath against the government with what he called a mere "whiff of grape-shot." As a result he was given command of the Army of the Interior. Subsequently he gained command of the French Army in Italy and succeeded in conquering the northern half of the country as well as forcing Austria into a peace treaty.

During the treaty negotiations, he held salons for generals and nobles. Congratulated on his success at one of these gatherings, he replied:

> What I have done so far is nothing. I am but at the opening of the career I have to run. Do you think that I have gained my victories in order to advance . . . the Directory? Do you think either that my object is to establish a republic? What a notion! What the French want is glory and the satisfaction of their vanity . . . the nation must have a head, a head who is rendered illustrious by glory and not by theories of government . . . or the talk of idealists.

The speaker was Napoleon Bonaparte. And it was this cal-culating man, this mocker of "theories of government," and "talk of idealists," who, in September, 1797, at the behest of the Directory, ordered the Prussian-Austrian Allies to free the idealistic political theorist, Lafayette. In view of Napoleon's victories, the Allies had no choice. The gates of Olmütz creaked open. But the gates of France remained closed. The Directory forbade Lafayette's return.

He went to the country home of a relative, the Countess de Tesse, at Wittmold, near what is today Hamburg, Germany, but was then southern Denmark. The Countess had fled

France in the early days of the revolution. Adrienne, who had been permitted to return to France, was agitating for similar permission for her husband. Meanwhile she sent the two girls to visit him at Wittmold. Georges, who had sailed home when his father was released, also visited whenever he got leave from Napoleon's army, which he had joined. Conveniently, his regiment was located in Holland. The two girls were delighted to be reunited with their brother, now nineteen and tall and handsome. Their admiration for him was unbounded. Anastasie, who had the habit of recording daily events in song much as other people might record them in a diary, wrote a new song for each of his visits. No matter that the words rarely fitted the music and that the rhyming was atrocious, the family applauded.

So did Charles La Tour Maubourg, a comrade of Georges, whose family were friends of his father. He and Anastasie fell head-over-heels in love. They were married May 5, 1798, in the chapel of the Countess de Tesse's estate, with much grumbling from the Countess, who called it "a peasant wedding." By her standards the courtship was too brief, the *trousseau* too small, the ceremony too informal. But Lafayette gave his blessing and the wedding was the way the two young lovers wanted—a most unusual circumstance for their times. The two bridesmaids were Virginie and Charles' sister.

Cheered by the wedding and the visits of the children, Lafayette began to mend his broken health at the Countess' rural retreat. He hoped to repair by his pen his equally shattered finances—at least to some extent. He set forth his philosophy of government, constitutional monarchy, in a small book called *The Royal Democracy*. Another slender volume followed, *Memories on Leaving Prison*. The latter included opinions on issues rarely even discussed in his time, though they are very current today. For example, on capital punishment: "No society has the right to take what it cannot give back." On prison as a corrective for crime: "The majority of

houses we call houses of correction are really places of de-
terioration far more likely to push criminals into the career
of vice and crime than to draw them out of it."

The books did nothing to assuage the uneasiness of Europe's rulers. Lafayette's former captors, in particular, de-
voutly hoped he would relieve them of his presence on the
continent by seeking asylum in that country of his heart,
America. Lafayette was as eager to go there as they were to
have him embark. He wrote Adrienne that he "would cross
the Atlantic in a balloon" if he thought the new American
administration would receive him. It would not. John Adams
had succeeded Washington in the Presidential office. And
John Adams wanted no part of Lafayette.

Sentiment in the United States, which had favored the
French Revolution at its start, had swung in the opposite di-
rection. The Reign of Terror had revolted the American
public and fear of the contagion of revolutionary violence
grew so strong that laws were passed making it more difficult for foreigners to apply for American citizenship and
easier for the government to send them home. The idea was
to reduce the foreign-born population. Other laws, doubtless
unconstitutional, imposed severe punishment for any criti-
cism of the government. Fortunately, the laws contained their
own termination date, which coincided with Adams's term.
They were the cause of near insurrection in two states, Virginia and Kentucky, and would probably have been repealed,
had they not included their own time limit. Congress later
made amends to those who had suffered under them.

This was the period during which Jefferson, a leader of the
Kentucky fight against the acts, was reviled as an atheist who
wished "to turn the United States over to a mob of murderous,
atheistical Jacobins." Since most of the foreigners who became American citizens joined the Republicans, Jefferson's
party, the Federalists, who were the opposing party, and
whose leadership included Adams, were eager to prevent

further swelling of Republican ranks. The debate over this issue was climaxing at the very moment when Lafayette was hoping for return to America. Besides this political strife, America's once warm relationship with France had cooled to the point where Congress had repealed the treaties which Lafayette and Jefferson had helped bring into being in 1778, and had authorized American ships to prey on French commerce. Eight thousand militia had been called up in readiness for war, with Washington in command.

In addition, the United States, a sensitive fledgling in the field of diplomacy, was miffed by the inattentive treatment American representatives received in France. The French, for their part, resented a treaty which America had signed with France's old enemy, England. No wonder that both Washington and Alexander Hamilton wrote Lafayette that the times were not propitious for him to visit the USA. Lafayette felt certain he could pour oil on these troubled waters and was disinclined to listen to the advice from his American friends that he should stay away. Had it not been for lack of money, he would probably have sailed in spite of their warnings.

Fortunately for the American–French relationship, and for Lafayette at this juncture—the man whose orders had liberated him from Olmütz became the instrument of a coup which, on November 10, 1799, put him in a position both to end the friction with the United States and to allow Lafayette to return to his own country.

Charles Maurice de Talleyrand, France's Minister of Foreign Affairs, was the mastermind of the coup. An unscrupulous but agile politician, he divided his talents about equally between the advancement of Talleyrand and the advancement of France. A bishop who was excommunicated for his efforts to establish a constitutional monarchy, he had fled first to England, then to the United States, returning to his own country with the advent of the Directory.

A firm believer in peace, he was intent on putting an end

to the Directory's wars, and a sound budget man, he lamented the Directory's disregard for inflation. He decided to replace it with a three-man Consulate and took steps toward that end. The First Consul, at least, he reasoned, must be a man of unstained image. Who came more naturally to mind than the young general who had followed his successes in Italy and Austria with a showy campaign in Egypt, aimed at weakening the British Empire? Not only did this man continue to win well-plotted victories; he forced losers to pay the costs, thus avoiding new burdens on French taxpayers. He also knew how and when to negotiate peace. When he returned to Paris from Egypt, he was a popular hero. The street where he lived, Chantereine, was renamed Rue de la Victoire—Street of Victory.

So Napoleon was propositioned. Three men called on him, at the behest of Talleyrand. They were the Minister of Police, Joseph Fouché, Roger Ducos, a director to remain as consul, and Emmanuel Sieyes. Sieyes was an old-time revolutionist who had aided Lafayette in the adoption of the Declaration of Rights. Now a director, he also would remain as a consul. Naturally, Napoleon accepted their invitation—but with one condition. He must not be thrust upon the people by force. The three-man Consulate must be chosen by the legislature. Sieyes took care of the upper house, where the vote went smoothly. The lower house, still controlled by the Jacobins, was more resistant. Its president, Lucien Bonaparte, Napoleon's brother, had to resort to a device to get the desired results. As president of the chamber, he had the right to call in troops. This he did, had them roll their drums and clear the hall. Then he reassembled those who would vote for the Consulate. The coup was complete.

Almost immediately after the coup, Adrienne called on the new first consul. She succeeded in obtaining from him permission for her husband to return to France. He had by this time left his aunt's estate and was attempting, without much success, to start a farm in Holland. Banned from France, unwanted in America, and regarded with suspicion throughout Europe, he was everywhere unwelcome, a man without a country. He had almost no money. He was clinging to existence by the claws of his willpower, when Adrienne's courier arrived, bringing him a passport to come home.

For the second time, Lafayette was in Napoleon's debt. And that was the way Napoleon wanted it. He believed Lafayette's reputation would be valuable to his purposes. Since the days when the new first consul had been a mere lieutenant in the French army, his confessed method of operation had been to imagine an ideal situation, then stop imagining and start calculating the moves required to make the ideal real. Lafayette, he hoped, could be used as one of the moves towards what he now had in mind. The exiled patriot's reputation for moral rectitude, his unquestionable devotion to the cause of liberty could provide precisely the camouflage needed by a man who dreamed of becoming emperor first of France, then of Europe.

# 6

---

# *The Emperor & the Castaway*

NAPOLEON reckoned without two other characteristics of Lafayette: indifference to reward other than the satisfaction of living up to his own standards, and a sense of values that left room for compromise only on those rare occasions when he could see tangible benefit for a greater goal.

When Lafayette first returned from prison and exile, he was prepared, even eager to assist in the government of reason which he wanted to believe Napoleon wished to inaugurate. In addition, he was grateful for the role Napoleon had played in his release, and therefore felt personally obligated to him.

The two men had long conversations in Napoleon's study, covering wide assortments of topics: the mistakes of the Revolution, the positions of church and state, the meaning of liberty and tyranny, the example of America. From these talks, as well as from interpreting events, Lafayette began to realize, well before other surviving revolutionaries, that Napoleon would never be a champion of the people.

"He draws the nation to him by the glamor and glory of his deeds, but he has no vision of a nation ruled by free institutions," Lafayette wrote Jefferson. He disapproved of the constitution drafted to meet the first consul's terms; it restricted electors of the Senate to five thousand; it limited freedom of the press. He expressed his objections freely to Napoleon, who, despite annoyance with Lafayette as "an impractical dreamer," had a grudging admiration for him. He was attracted by the very steadfastness that irritated him. Lafayette was, in turn, "more attracted than I ought to be by a despot." He was fascinated by Napoleon's ability to analyze people and situations, and by the elasticity of his mind. In one of their conversations he told Napoleon that the consul could have been a Washington had he so chosen. Napoleon laughed. "You understand the American Presidency would never go down here," he replied.

"No," Lafayette snapped, "you would have had to forego pomp and guards." Napoleon appreciated the frankness. To an advisor who criticized his association with Lafayette he answered. "He has never said anything behind my back that he has not said to my face. Can you say as much for yourself?"

When Napoleon offered Lafayette the ambassadorship to the United States, Lafayette refused gracefully, saying, "I am too much of an American to live in the United States as a foreigner." In his refusal of a seat in the Senate, subsequently offered, he was more blunt:

> From the direction which public affairs are taking, what I already see and it is easy to foresee, it does not seem suitable to my character to enter into an order of things contrary to my principles and in which I have to contend, without public utility, against a man to whom I am indebted for great obligations.

At this time he announced his intention to retire from the army, on the pretext that his place should be open for a younger man. Napoleon gave him an annual pension of six thousand francs (a little over a thousand dollars), which he accepted as his due for past military services. Napoleon's service, he would not enter.

Nevertheless, the conversational duels between the two continued for a couple of years, giving stimulation to both, though neither would budge an inch from his own position.

An incident which strained the relationship between the two men took place when Napoleon's brother, Joseph, invited Lafayette to dine at his home with Cornwallis. Lafayette had cherished no grudge against the defeated British general, and found the invitation amusing. In response to some teasing questions from Cornwallis at the dinner table, he spoke eloquently for the need for more representative government in France. Cornwallis repeated these remarks to Napoleon who opened his next conversation with Lafayette by saying, "Lord Cornwallis pretends that you are not yet reformed."

"Reformed from what?" asked Lafayette. "From loving liberty? From hating the crimes of terrorist tyranny? I only hate them more and more and hold all the more to my principles."

"I must tell you, General Lafayette, that your manner of expressing yourself lends the weight of your name to the enemies of my government," Napoleon warned.

"What do you want me to do?" retorted Lafayette. "I live in retreat in the country; I avoid speechmaking, but whenever someone asks me if your government conforms to my ideas of liberty, I reply, no, for, in the final analysis, General, I wish to be very prudent, but I will not be a renegade."

Finally an issue arose, as it was bound to do, which snapped entirely the weakening relationship. As first consul, Napoleon had made the Tuileries his residence. Moving in, he had said, "It's not the whole thing to be at the Tuileries. The trick is to stay there." To insure his stay he requested the nation in 1802 to make him consul for life, with the right to choose his successor. The request was in the form of a nationwide plebiscite in which the people could vote yes or no. The result: three and a half million said yes, eight thousand, no. Napoleon had been sure the plebiscite would go his way; otherwise he would not have attempted it. As the Swedish ambassador to France wrote home: "A legitimate monarch has perhaps never found a people more willing to do his bidding than Bonaparte . . . France will perform the impossible in order to aid him."

His popularity had a pocketbook base. The French had much more to thank him for than the "glory" earned by his military victories. In the period of peace these victories bought, he had rebuilt commerce and put banking on its feet. He had repaired old roads and built new ones and reopened the inter-river canal system which weeds had choked during the revolution. Once more laden barges plied north, south, east and west. The Napoleonic network of transport enriched national markets with the products of a revival in manufacturing which he had encouraged and nourished. Similar distribution of agricultural bounty pleased both farmer and consumer. Two years of Napoleon, and France was in economic balance for the first time in two hundred years.

For every segment of the population Napoleon had something. The emigrés were pardoned and allowed to return. The churches were given back to the church, the loyalty oath abolished. A uniform system of law—the Napoleonic Code—established equal justice for all citizens in civil, commercial and criminal matters. Of most of these changes Lafayette approved. What he could not brook was that in the final analysis the reins of government ended in the grip of one virtually self-appointed citizen. His vote in the plebiscite was one of the eight thousand no's. He wrote on his ballot, "I cannot vote for such a magistrature until public liberty is sufficiently guaranteed; then I shall give my voice for Napoleon Bonaparte." Wishing to make his views perfectly clear to Napoleon himself, he wrote a letter addressed not to the Consul, but to the general:

When a man who is deeply impressed with a sense of the gratitude he owes you . . . connects his suffrage with conditional restrictions, these restrictions amply prove that no one will more gladly than himself see you the chief magistrate . . . of a free republic. . . . In your consular authority there was . . . discerned that dictatorial prerogative which, under the auspices of your genius accomplished such glorious purposes; yet less glorious than the restoration of liberty . . . It is not possible, General, that you, who are the first amidst that order of mankind who surveys every age and every country before the status of its members can be determined, can desire that a revolution marked by so many victories and so much blood, so many sufferings and valiant deeds, have for you and the world no other result than an arbitrary regime. The French people have too long known their rights to forget them forever; though perhaps they are nearer recovering them and enjoying them now than under the period of revolutionary effervescence. And you, by the force of your character and the influence of public confidence, by the superiority of your talents, your power and your fortune, are able to reestablish liberty, subdue all dangers and calm anxieties. . . .

I have then only patriotic and personal motives in desiring for you the completion of your glory, a permanent government; but the principles, engagements and actions of my entire life demand that I await before giving my voice for it, the knowledge that your authority is erected on a basis worthy of the nation and yourself. I hope, General, that you will recognize here, as you have done on all other occasions, a steady continuance of my political opinions, combined with sincere wishes for your personal welfare.

Napoleon didn't answer the letter. But when his ministers congratulated him on the vote, discounting the small opposition as probably representing only die-hard Jacobins, he disagreed. "No," he said, "there were some that arose from enthusiasm for liberty; Lafayette's, for example."

About a month after Napoleon became first consul, George Washington died. Napoleon ordered a day of mourning throughout France. In Paris he issued invitations to a memorial service in Les Invalides. No member of the Lafayette family received one. Georges, however, insisted on attending. A murmur of shock rippled through the assemblage as he defiantly took a seat. But no one attempted to oust him.

To Lafayette it was quite clear that no useful place for him or his family would ever exist in Napoleon's Paris. He retired to La Grange, a chateau recently inherited by his wife, some thirty miles northeast of Paris. Referring to himself as the *naufragé,* the castaway, he divided his time between farming, attempting to repair his shattered fortune, correspondence with his American friends and entertaining the French liberals and foreign admirers who shared his persistent optimism that "Those Rights of Mankind, which, in 1789, have been the blessings of the end of the last century, shall before the end of the present one be the undisputed creed and insured property not only of this, but of every European nation."

In 1804, Napoleon went on from the consulate to crown himself emperor in the cathedral of Notre Dame. He had prepared for the step with another plebiscite (three and one half million in favor, twenty-five hundred opposed). In that plebiscite Lafayette refused to vote at all. He remained silent at La Grange. But the silence didn't deceive the man who had all France except Lafayette and a handful of faithful Fayettists. Napoleon rarely mentioned his former admonitor, but one day he said to a minister, "All have been reformed—save only one—Lafayette. He has never flinched from his conviction. You see him quiet. Well, I am telling you, he is entirely ready to begin all over again."

Napoleon's prophecy was right, though some years would pass before it would be fulfilled. The emperor and the castaway understood each other well. For his part, Napoleon was never able to overcome a rankling resentment of Lafayette's indifference to the lures with which he was accustomed to attract his followers. Lafayette was the one gem missing in the imperial crown, "the only man of the revolution who could not be bought," he observed bitterly. Whenever opportunity arose, he gave vent to his grudge. Lafayette's son, Georges Washington, was recommended for army promotion by his general. Napoleon turned down the recommendation and eventually forced both Georges and the Marquis de Lasteyrie, whom Virginie had by that time married, out of the service. He even tried—unsuccessfully—to have Lafayette named as a conspirator in an assassination plot.

Lafayette brushed off such incidents. He emerged from La Grange only for annual visits to Chavaniac, for business errands in Paris and on Bastille day, July 14th, when he was invariably called upon to make commemorative speeches hither and yon. In these he discussed the state of liberty around the world. The rising revolts against Spain in South America was one favorite theme, the abolition of serfdom and social classes in Prussia was another. Only by implication did he reflect on the state of liberty in France. "We may conclude that if liberty too often meets with rocks and stoppages, at other times it finds its way unexpectedly," he would sum up, inferring that the stoppage was French, the progress foreign. His consciousness of his moral obligation to the Emperor prevented him from more specific comment.

Only to Jefferson, by then President of the United States, did he unburden himself, describing Napoleon as "a singular genius, disharmonized by the folly of ambition, the immorality of his mind, and this grain of madness not incompatible with great talents." Jefferson, who not only distrusted but despised Napoleon, replied with greater vehemence:

I turn from the contemplation [of Napoleon] with loath-
ing and take refuge in the histories of other times . . . We
are comforted with the reflection that the condemnation
[of tyrants] by all succeeding generations has confirmed the
censures of the historians and consigned their memories to
everlasting infamy, a solace we have with the Georges and
Napoleons . . . [only] by anticipation.

Shortly after the United States purchased Louisiana from
France in 1803, Jefferson wrote Lafayette to sound out
whether he would accept the governorship of the new territory were it offered to him. Lafayette replied with a short note
which said neither yes or no. Not until three months later did
he write a long refusal which contained perhaps the clearest
analysis he ever made of his own political vision:

I readily acknowledge that in our going to Louisiana . . .
there is for me, and there alone perhaps can be expected,
the reunion of dignity, wealth and safety. Nor am I less
animated than thirty years ago by the idea to walk along
with American liberty in her progress throughout the continent, where to be employed in her service . . . would
render the end of my life happy as the begginning
[*sic.*] . . .
Yet, my dear friend, you also have been a witness and
partaker in my expectations of French and of course European liberty. In America the cause of mankind is won
and assured. . . . Here it is reckoned to be lost and ir-
retrievable. But to pronounce its doom to myself, to pro-
claim it, as it were, by a final expatriation, is a concession
so repugnant to my nature that unless I am quite forced
to it . . . I don't know how the hope, however faint it is,
can be totally abandoned. Amidst the usurpations of un-
controuled [*sic.*] power, and in case of a fall [of the French
government] the probable dangers from enraged Jacobins,
the now still greater ones from a royal aristocracy . . . I
will not despair of modifications less unfavorable to the

dignity and freedom of my countrymen. And while I consider the prodigious influence of French doctrines on the
future destinies of the world, I persuade myself that I, a
promoter of this revolution, must not acknowledge the impossibility to see it, in our days, restored on its true basis of
generous, upright, and in one word, American liberty. . . .

Hitherto I have kept clear of public employments . . .
I am loath to meddle with an administration so countrary
[*sic.*] to my constant professed doctrine. In Department
cases, I restrict myself to polite pretenses, while in offers
of more important nature, I have answered the friends of
government and Bonaparte himself that a life of retirement was my determined choice. The matter of the consulate for life, in which I declared that I was waiting to give
him my vote until public liberty was sufficiently guaranteed, has put an end to my communication with him . . .
In the imperial business, I refrained from voting. The last
news I had of him and probably from him was that my retirement was entirely the result of my enimity [*sic.*] toward
him and his government, I answered that as to him I was
aware of confered [*sic.*] . . . obligations, but that . . . to
an absolute government I could not be a friend.

Adieu my dear, respected, excellent friend. I am, with
every sentiment of affection, gratitude and regard, your
obliged, loving friend,

Lafayette

Earlier in this letter, Lafayette had explained the reason
for his delay in replying to Jefferson's query. During the
previous winter he had slipped on the ice and fractured his
thigh. Doctors feared that he would be lame for life. One of
them, a Doctor Boyer, had just invented a mechanism to
create traction. Lafayette agreed to try it. A clumsy metal instrument was strapped tightly around his leg. He soon developed sores; the sores became infected. Pus oozed from
under the metal. Still the doctor left the device in place.

Meanwhile Virginie's wedding to the Marquis de Lasteyrie

was being delayed until her father could attend. When the physician acknowledged he could not predict when that would be, the family decided to hold the wedding in the room next to Lafayette's, with the door flung wide between.

His daughter's apparent happiness was the only joy Lafayette experienced during what he described as forty days and forty nights of "the maximum of pain a human body can support." When the device was removed, a part of his leg, rotted with gangrene, came off with it. His hip was permanently stiffened. He had to learn to walk all over again.

When Jefferson's letter arrived, Lafayette was about to leave with Adrienne for a sojourn at Mont-Dore in Auvergne, a site where hot springs were shadowed by the massive Puy de Sancy whose majesty Lafayette loved. The spring waters were prescribed for the rehabilitation of injured joints and muscles. Evidently the treatment helped him regain mobility, for he told Jefferson that he "derived much benefit" and intended to return. He also told him that Adrienne was taken "greviously ill" on the homeward journey, and by the time the couple reached Chavaniac, where they were due for a stopover, a physician had to be called.

The physician was not hopeful. Adrienne had never fully recovered from the effects of the scurvy she had contracted in prison. She was anemic and she had developed an ulcer. She had managed to hide her worsening condition from her husband and children, but after the Mont-Dore attack it could no longer be concealed. She declined steadily until she became a total invalid. In the fall of 1807, she was taken to Paris, ravaged by fever and babbling in delirium.

One effect of delirium was to unshackle emotions for her husband which she had kept under control during thirty-four years of married life, for fear of distressing him. Lafayette later recalled how she had drawn him down to her bed, fondling him and hugging him with amazing force for one so wasted. "I love you," she told him, "with all my body."

On Christmas Eve the delirium subsided. Her clarity and control returned. She began to recite the Canticle of Tobias, the same psalm she had recited on her way to share Lafayette's dungeon. Her voice grew faint, wound down and stopped. Then, seeming to muster all the strength that remained to her, she said to the family surrounding her bed, "I wish you the peace of the Lord," adding in a whisper to Lafayette whose hand she had been clutching, "I am all yours." She always had been.

Never before had Lafayette been personally hurt by the irreparable loss of someone close to him. His experiences with death had been mainly on the battlefield and were a customary part of a soldier's life. When a daughter had died, he had been wrapped up in the conduct of the American Revolution. He was almost as unaware of her death as he had been of her short life. His mother and grandfather had played brief roles in his existence; no deep bonds had been severed by their deaths. He remembered the death of his soldier father only as an event to make the English enemy pay for. Now he was face-to-face with death as a personal grievance, a finality that could not be reversed. Adrienne, whom he had come to love so late in their marriage, but so deeply, was gone. For good. There it was.

There had been a time when her death might have made as scant impression on him as the others in his life. But all that had changed at Olmütz. In the words of the wife of Lafayette's aide-de-camp, Fanny d'Arblay: "Though her virtues and conduct had always been objects to him of respect and esteem, he became, by universal account, far more warmly . . . attached to . . . the wife who had followed him into captivity . . . than he had ever been formerly."

His usual attitude of "if-I-had-to-do-it-all-over-again-I-would-do-it-the-same-way" was defeated by her death. Unburdening his heart to Jefferson he wrote, "Before this blow, I confess I did not know what it was to be unhappy. There was hitherto no effort in my standing superior to all vicissitudes. Now I feel myself irresistably overpowered." To an old companion of the De la Tour Maubourg family into which daughter Anastasie had married, he added, "Until now you have found me stronger than any circumstance; today, circumstance is stronger than I." He had discovered that man is by no means the sole director of his fate.

He was also having his first experience with guilt. He told Jefferson that he feared Adrienne's "life had been . . . shortened by her married existence." Full of regrets, he, who had so often during Adrienne's life left her to pursue his own ideals, refused during her dying to leave her bedside. He even became, as he admitted to Maubourg, jealous of others' attentions to her. "I confess," he said, "that for the first time in my . . . married life, I experienced a feeling of jealousy."

After the funeral he locked her room and permitted no one but himself to go in. He celebrated her birthday, annually, by remaining all day in her room, alone. Night and day, around his neck he wore her picture and a strand of her hair in a locket. But his life, though stripped of Adrienne's presence and tortured with grief, was not lonely. La Grange had become a mecca for surviving liberals, not only French, but British. Distinguished guests flocked there in droves. Charles Fox, now again British Foreign Secretary, and his nephew, the Lord Privy Seal, Henry Holland, whose salon at Holland House in London was the forum of Britain's free-thinking intellectuals, visited frequently at La Grange. So did the Scottish Whig leader, James Lauderdale, and the great trial lawyer, Thomas Erskine, famed defender of English radicals under fire for their sympathies with the French Revolution. Their host, who had once hated England as much as he loved America and France, now found in the company of these brilliant men a kinship of spirit which strengthened his growing conviction that "the contest between special privileges and universal rights" was universal and must be universally waged.

The English guests mingled with French writers and journalists like Madame de Staël, who told Lafayette, "I shall always have hope for the human race as long as you exist." With Madame de Staël came her lover, the political theorist and pamphleteer, Benjamin Constant. From time to time men belonging to reformist groups in Portugal, Spain and Germany joined the ever widening circle at La Grange. It was not unusual, Madame de Staël related, for forty people, including Lafayette's three children, his sons- and daughter-in-law, and nine grandchildren to be seated at the dinner table.

He made a custom of sitting between two of the grandchildren, a different pair each night. Georges' three girls, Nathalie, Mathilde and Clementine; Anastasie's daughters Celestine, Louise and Jenny; Virginie's son Jules and his sisters Pauline and Mélanie all took turns sitting on either side of their grandfather. In later years three more would be added to the fold. "I believe one is never too young to be introduced to the necessity for liberty," he insisted. And indeed the conversation concentrated on that necessity. Various schemes were proposed to promote pan-European progress in human rights, for example a union of British, Irish, French and Dutch patriots. There was even talk of a United States of Europe to replace national governments. Often the discussions continued in the drawing room until ten, Lafayette's bedtime. As the guests rose from the table, the talk broadened. One cluster of conversationalists would take off on the need for abolition of slavery; another might delve into prison reform. These were favorite topics. Lafayette moved from group to group, listening here, contributing a thought there. And so, at ten, to bed. Ideas would flow again tomorrow.

Far from being a forgotten man in his retirement, Lafayette had become the unofficial chairman of a continuing revolutionary think tank, word of which soon reached Napoleon. Publicly, he discounted the participants as impractical "ideologues." Privately, he was irked by the ferment he knew the conversations kept alive, no matter how removed from the center of power the ideologues might be. "Lafayette is the only one who clings obstinately to the principles of liberty," he told his brother, Joseph, "and what is more, he is preparing for their restoration." He was haunted, justifiably, by the fear that Lafayette's concept of right could eventually defeat his own reliance on might.

Napoleon's comment to Joseph was reported to Lafayette who quoted it in a letter to Jefferson on July 4, 1812. Reminiscing on the significance of the month of July as the beginning of both the American and French Revolutions, he harked back to the signing of the Declaration of Independence thirty-six years earlier, then added:

> In other times you have seen me full of hope for France in this same month of July, and you approved my Declaration of Rights, whose effect we thought would be as durable as it was decisive. Nevertheless, whatever the violation and corruption of it, and . . . whatever the determined prohibition of liberal thinking, I am convinced that those principles are more alive than one might think and that they will again rule the old world as they now rule the new one.

If Adrienne's death had taken from him his naïve faith in man's ability to direct his immediate destiny, it had not injured his abiding belief in a final triumph of justice over tyranny even if, as Fox once told him, "we do not see that in our lifetime." Fox had added, "Surely either Georges will see it, or at least his children." This was the extension of Fayettism into the future.

Both Napoleon and Lafayette saw the gatherings at La Grange as nourishing that future "like a foetus" as Thomas Erskine put it. Madame de Staël was more elegant. "La Grange is to the nineteenth century what the Benedictines were to the fifteenth," she declared one evening at dinner. The Benedictines were the principal religious order of the

Middle Ages engaged in preserving the culture that blossomed into the Renaissance.

Perhaps the simplicity of the fare at La Grange contributed to the display of intellect. The food was plenteous, but plain, being homegrown on the five hundred acres which Lafayette cultivated on the eight-hundred-acre estate. Beef and milk came from the thirty to forty head of panda-faced Marron cows, a Norman species, plus others from England and Switzerland. His smokehouse was well hung with hams and sides of bacon, the pigs having been a gift from the city of Baltimore. His Merino sheep, of which he was particularly proud since he was the first to introduce this breed in France, numbered one thousand. A large fishpond, dotted with tiny islands, was kept well-stocked.

His fields, used largely for pasturage and livestock feed, rippled in summer with crops of corn, hay and alfalfa, and his vegetable garden produced hefty harvests of potatoes and beets. Pear and apple trees—the latter lining the long driveway to the chateau—were heavily weighted with fruit in fall. At that season too, the wine grapes were gathered from his ample vineyards. The entire vintage was sold. The ever abstemious Lafayette now served no wine at all at his table. Fall was also wood cutting time. Come winter, logs from La Grange's forest would crackle and snap in the chateau fireplaces.

To manage the work calendar for this sizable estate, Lafayette was fortunate in having an excellent overseer, by the name of Lescuyer. Lescuyer was also an auditor with a scrupulous eye for detail. In his books every item, down to · the last jug of milk, the last jar of jam, was entered and accounted for. Owner and overseer worked well together with the score of regularly employed farmhands, a staff which quadrupled at harvest time. The only disagreements between the two arose from Lafayette's generosity.

He refused to prefer charges against workers who cut his

wood for their own hearths. He gave away two hundred pounds of bread every Monday, triple that much in times of scarcity, accompanied by soup. One year, when scarcities were very great, Lescuyer warned that there would be nothing left for the chateau if Lafayette kept giving away his produce. "There is a very simple way of solving this problem," Lafayette replied. "By retiring to Chavaniac we may abandon to the poor what we would have consumed by remaining at La Grange. Their existence will thus be prolonged until harvest time." Lescuyer shook his head. This was not his idea of how to do business. But it was the one issue on which Lafayette, usually receptive to Lescuyer's every suggestion, refused to give an inch. When cholera struck in the region, he and his whole family volunteered as nurses. He spent thirty-eight thousand francs ($7,150) to employ doctors and purchase medicine.

On Sunday evenings the entire staff, farm workers and chateau servants alike, were invited to dance in the dining room. The gate porter supplied the music with his violin. After the dance, cakes and sugar water were served. Lafayette always hosted these occasions himself. One of his daughters acted as hostess, pouring the sugar water and passing the cakes.

The next morning—back to work as usual. Speaking through a megaphone from the window of his second floor apartment, Lafayette issued his orders to the laborers gathered below. Immediately after lunch he drove a light caleche around his acres to inspect the work. He would have preferred to walk; at first he did, but after his leg injury he was forced to rely on a cane and could no longer walk that far. One of his pleasures on these inspection trips was his menagerie where he kept animals sent him as presents from abroad. Another was his stable where his white horse was stalled. Gradually, he was learning to ride again.

The rest of the day, until dinnertime, was given over to

paperwork. He awakened regularly at 5:00 A.M. and worked in bed on his memoirs and correspondence. After giving workers their instructions, he read newspapers until lunch. The apartment where he worked was crowded with Americana. On the walls hung engravings of the Declaration of Independence and Washington's farewell address, along with gravures of Washington, Franklin, Jefferson and Madison. Later he added Andrew Jackson to the gallery. There was a portrait of his Maryland host, Francis Huger, and busts of James Monroe and John Adams. There was a picture of the Spanish port from which he had embarked on his first voyage to America. On his bed the pillow was covered with a tapestry slip showing various types of shells. It had been woven for him by Martha Washington. The walls of the vestibule leading into his bedroom were draped with flags which had been flown at various crucial moments in his life, both in America and France. There was also a reminder of the grim days at Olmütz. Anastasie had recreated her thumbnail caricature of their prison guard and it hung in his anteroom.

When he emerged from work to greet his guests, the figure they saw showed signs of the wear and tear of recent years. Physical inaction, forced by his injury, had let him accumulate weight. Heaviness coarsened the cameo-like feature of his face and thickened the frame of his body. His eyelids were beginning to crease and pouches were deepening beneath his eyes. The nipped waistline had given way to portliness. "His appearance has altered," commented Fanny d'Arblay, "but he is a mellower man for it—more amiable by far."

The gentle panorama at La Grange differed diametrically from the stark vistas of Chavaniac. Did Lafayette prefer these softer surroundings as he aged? Probably not, for as he had once said, Auvergne was in his bones and blood. But there were advantages, especially for a lame man, in being so near Paris. Not only could he reach the city more easily when necessary; it was also easier for the guests who provided his intellectual stimulation to reach him. Moreover he had La Grange to himself and the immediate family he enjoyed having around him. Aged relatives lived in Chavaniac, to one of whom, his aunt, he finally sold his childhood home, being desperately in need of money.

Money was the one problem that pressed in on the edges of Lafayette's orderly, uncomplicated life at La Grange. He had never paid a great deal of attention to his financial affairs; he was not, as Lescuyer could have testified, a budget-minded man. He had inherited a more than comfortable fortune, but he had spent large sums of it (the equivalent of $200,000) on the American Revolution, and a considerable amount on his National Guard during the French Revolution. Moreover, he always found it difficult, if not impossible, to resist aiding those who had less than he. As a result, his income in 1802 was reduced to the equivalent of $1,500 a year and his debts amounted to $50,000. His creditors were understandably impatient.

A former aide-de-camp of Lafayette's, Bureaux Pusy, quietly put in process the means to bail his old commander out of trouble. Pusy had married the stepdaughter of Dupont de Nemours, a French economist and revolutionary theorist who was a good friend of Jefferson's. Shortly after his marriage, Pusy settled in America. With an introduction from his father-in-law, he made Jefferson's acquaintance and hastened to inform him of Lafayette's plight. Jefferson promptly instructed American representatives in Paris to look into the matter. They confirmed Pusy's story, but added that it would be difficult to persuade Lafayette to accept financial help as he preferred to keep his problems to himself. Meanwhile, Dupont de Nemours had suggested to Jefferson a special resolution of the United States Congress calling for reimbursement of half of what Lafayette had spent on the American Revolution, an itemized account of which Dupont included in his letter.

Jefferson felt this suggestion was awkward. It required an appropriation no other American army officer had ever received. The precedent could cause trouble in Congress and in the army, let alone causing embarrassment for Lafayette. After some study, he came up with a more suitable idea. At the end of the revolution, Congress had passed an act enabling veterans to receive land grants, the size dependent on rank and terms of service. Lafayette, though notified of this opportunity, had failed to take advantage of it and the time limit for doing so had long expired. However, to ask Congress for an extension of that limit seemed plausible. Such an act was passed by a unanimous vote in both houses.

The location of the land grant selected by Jefferson at Lafayette's request, was in the new American territory of Louisiana. It was acreage which could demand a good market price, providing Lafayette not only with the means to pay off his debts, but also supplying him with a source of income. However, there were hitches that Jefferson had not foreseen. The city of New Orleans claimed rights to a certain part of the grant and a private individual, a Mr. John Gravier, to other parts. Obviously the land could not be sold for any suitable price, nor could funds be borrowed on it as security when the ownership, or title was disputed.

Meanwhile, Lafayette had become desperate enough to confess to Jefferson in 1810 that he was "on the brink of ruin." Only with great difficulty did Jefferson persuade him not to sell the grant cheaply to speculators willing to take the risk of an uncleared title. Finally in May, 1812, the title was cleared for part of the land, due largely to the efforts of James Madison, then President of the United States, whom Jefferson constantly prodded on the matter. In 1814, the remainder of the grant was freed from other claims and sold. Lafayette was able to write Jefferson, "Thanks to the munificence of Congress and the kindness of my friends, I am now perfectly clear of debts and pecuniary embarrassment. I feel a grateful satisfaction in giving you the pleasure to hear it."

The satisfaction marked a reversal of the tide of Lafayette's life. Once more it was rising, not with any sudden rush as in the early days of the Revolution of 1789, but with slow wave after wave of events carrying the castaway to new shores.

The emperor, whom Lafayette had characterized as a "despot" and a man having "no vision of a nation ruled by free institutions" had finally let his ambition push him beyond the bounds of reason. In 1806, England, nervous at the extent of Napoleon's conquests of other European nations, had blockaded the whole northern coast of the continent. Retaliating, Napoleon had forbidden commerce with England throughout the continental territory he controlled. Within a few years the prosperity Napoleon had given France began to weaken. Trade was shackled. At the same time, to the south, in Spain, the people rebelled against Napoleon's brother Joseph, whom he had installed on the throne. The open revolt was quickly quenched but guerrilla warfare continued. Joseph's throne was shaky.

Discontent rumbled through the empire like the herald of a storm. Perhaps louder than anybody, Napoleon heard the storm warnings. The most ominous came from a new ally he had cultivated—Russia. Not only did Russia object strenuously to the British blockade; she also protested Napoleon's takeover and partitioning of neighboring Poland. He decided to silence this loud critic, Russia, as an example to the others. He reasoned that her defeat would restore the prestige essential to his concept of government.

In May, 1812, he set out with four hundred thousand men to subdue Moscow. The Russians led him a four months' dance of death, enticing him ever deeper into terrain which they had devastated in advance. Napoleon was prevented from following his usual procedure of commandeering food from the conquered. There was no food to be commandeered. And all along the march, guerrillas harassed his ever-hungrier army.

In September, the Russians feinted a formal stand. Napoleon defeated them, and, cheered by the defeat, persevered on toward Moscow. The weather grew colder and colder. Three-quarters of the army died from exposure or starvation. But the remaining quarter, cheered by their general, looked forward to warmth and food in Moscow. They found neither. The Russians had burned the city before Napoleon's arrival. He was forced to lead his soldiers home, in what was more of a rout than a retreat. Only twenty thousand of the original four hundred thousand made it to Paris.

Napoleon had gone too far for a man of his personality to stop. He was determined to wipe out the Russian smirch on his brilliant military record. He raised a new army of six hundred thousand, including men formerly considered too old or too young for conscription. Back to Russia!

The new army never even reached the Russian border. Prussia and Austria allied themselves with Russia and in a three-day battle near Leipzig, Germany, October 16 to 19, 1813, they defeated the emperor.

Before the year was out, Prussia, Austria, England, the German States over which Napoleon held the title Protector, and Spain joined the Alliance. On March 31, 1814, the Allies marched into Paris, demanding that Napoleon give up his throne—abdicate. Lafayette, at La Grange, locked himself in his apartment and wept—not for Napoleon, but for subjugated France. The map of Europe was redrawn by the Allies, meeting amid much gaiety in Vienna to divide the spoils as they saw fit, without reference to the wishes or needs of the affected populations. Of their Congress Lafayette said, "The only good thing the Congress of Vienna ever did was to abolish the slave trade. We who worked for abolition forty years earlier were considered visionaries. In another forty years, people will not understand how such an infamous trade could ever have been tolerated."

In France the imperious Louis XVIII, brother of the guillotined Louis XVI, was crowned king. He was a man blinded to the temper of the times by royal breeding. He considered his coronation merely a confirmation of his rights to the throne since the boyhood execution of the prince who would have been Louis XVII. He signed his documents with the date "In the nineteenth year of our reign." Lafayette went briefly to Paris, but was not welcome at Louis's court, dominated by royalists and former supporters of Napoleon. The only force these two groups hated worse than they hated each other was the force of Lafayette's anti-one-man-government convictions. Just as well pleased to be snubbed, Lafayette returned to La Grange. He sensed, as he wrote Jefferson that Louis's determination to turn the clock back to pre-Revolutionary days would be checkmated "by the people themselves." At that point he would be ready to help.

He hadn't long to wait. The ambitions of Napoleon had trod on the toes of other European nations, not on the toes of the French. Louis walked on the revolution and the people would not put up with that. A growing majority longed for Napoleon's return from the island of Elba to which the Allies had exiled him. On the streets of Paris his supporters coined a password: "Do you believe in Jesus Christ?" The answer: "Yes, and in his resurrection." Word was sent to the exile that unless he returned, someone else would be certain to seize power.

The message was enough to resurrect the emperor. On March 7, 1815, representatives of the nations included in the Congress of Vienna were attending a fancy dress ball in that city. As the strains of the last waltz wafted to a conclusion, a courier from the King of Sardinia arrived with an electrifying message. "The man" had landed in France and was marching on Paris. Actually, he had landed on March 1st. Gathering an army as he marched, he arrived in Paris and moved into the Tuileries two weeks later. Louis had fled.

The time for which Lafayette waited had come. Napoleon,

grasping at straws now, swallowed his emnity and offered Lafayette a seat as first member of the peerage in the upper house of the Assembly, composed of the nobility. This, in keeping with his principles, Lafayette refused. Instead he ran for and won a seat from the La Grange district, Seine-et-Marne, in the lower chamber, the Chamber of Deputies. To his astonishment after his years of absence from political life, he found himself among friends. Promptly the deputies chose him as one of their four vice-presidents. Old-time rabid Jacobins, mellowed by the disastrous results of their ruthless policies, crowded around him to shake hands. The moderation for which he had once been mocked had become the political creed of all but a handful of Bonapartist or die-hard royalist deputies.

Napoleon attended the ceremonies of the opening session. Afterward he and Lafayette met briefly on their way out. Dignified in his toga-like imperial robes, even though lined and jowly of face, paunchy and flabby of figure, the emperor stopped and stared at Lafayette. Here was the master of the one will in France he had never been able to bend. Lafayette returned the gaze steadily. The emperor broke the silence. "The country air has done you good," he said. "It has, Sire," Lafayette replied. That was all.

Two weeks later, Lafayette put in motion the parliamentary process which would end in demand for the emperor's second abdication. The background for it was Waterloo. There on June 18, 1815, Napoleon attacked British forces commanded by the Duke of Wellington. Wellington's troops were soon reinforced by Prussians under General Gebhard Blucher. Napoleon was roundly defeated and the French army streamed back toward Paris with Wellington in pursuit.

Rumors preceded the army, the strongest of which was that Napoleon intended to dissolve the Assembly. This was, in fact, his intention. Only a dictatorship, he believed, could cope with the military crisis which threatened France's extinction as a European power. When Lafayette heard of Napoleon's plans from the Chief of Police, Joseph Fouché, he immediately notified the Assembly. An eyewitness described the scene:

> He spoke as conversationally as though he were in the drawing room. The silence in the Assembly was absolute. He proposed a resolution:
> "Whereas the Chamber of Deputies declares that the independence of the nation is threatened, be it resolved that the Chamber declares itself to be in permanent session, and that any attempt to dissolve it is a crime of high treason. . . . And be it further resolved that the Minister of the Interior is invited to muster and arm the National Guard and the Ministers of War, Foreign Affairs and the Interior and Police are invited to come immediately to the Assembly."

The resolution was adopted without a single dissent. The summoned ministers arrived shortly, accompanied by Napoleon's brother, Lucien. Lucien lashed out bitterly, accusing France of being a weak nation, incapable of endurance and perseverance. Lafayette replied in sword-edged accents:

> Prince, this is a calumny. By what right do you dare to accuse the nation of . . . want of perseverance in the emperor's interest? The nation has followed him on the fields of Italy, over the burning sands of Egypt, in the immense plains of Germany, across the frozen deserts of Russia . . . The nation has followed him in fifty battles, in his defeats as in his victories, and in so doing we have to mourn the blood of three million Frenchmen."

Lucien didn't even try to reply. When he reported the tenor of the speech and the mood of the Assembly to Napoleon, the Emperor said, "I knew I ought to have got rid of these people before I left. It is the end. They will ruin France."

It was truly the end for Napoleon. In the afternoon a committee of thirty—the ministers, the presidents and vice-presidents of the Chamber of Deputies and other officers of state —met in the Tuileries. Lafayette proposed that they go as a group to the Emperor to demand his abdication. The committee was afraid of taking the responsibility for such action, though every member agreed that it was necessary. The following day, member after member of the Chamber, disgusted by the committee's cowardice, rose to demand abdication. News arrived that the Emperor would refuse. Lafayette, backed by the Chamber, sent him an ultimatum: "Abdicate or be dethroned."

An hour later, Napoleon gave in. But he refused to surrender to the chamber. He made his way to Rochefort, where he gave himself up to the English who were blockading that western port.

To the day he died on the distant island of Saint Helena, to which the Allies exiled him, his bitterness against what he called Lafayette's "vague ideas of liberty, undigested and ill thought-out," never mellowed. Writing his memoirs in his last years, he stated emphatically, "His (Lafayette's) arousing of the chamber after Waterloo lost us everything."

It won Lafayette nothing. Fouché, noted for fancy footwork in jumping from sinking stars to rising ones, got himself appointed by the Chamber of Deputies as head of a provisional government. He then located the self-exiled Louis XVIII and persuaded the Assembly to put him back on the throne, his authority limited, however, by a charter guaranteeing elections and civil rights. At Fouché's behest, Lafayette was sent to settle the peace terms with the victorious Allies, a thankless task which kept him absent from the Assembly, which was just where Fouché wanted him—out of the way.

By the time Lafayette regained political stride, royalists, with Fouché's conniving, were in control of the Assembly. When Lafayette rose to speak, they tried to drown him out.

But the galleries, packed with his supporters, drowned out the royalists. Lafayette waited silently until the contest ceased, taking a pinch of snuff. Apparently unconcerned by the hullabaloo, his attitude suggested "why all this fuss about me?" When quiet returned he picked up the threads of his speech, always a thundering attack on royalist violations of the Charter, especially the undermining of the free press.

To counter royalist moves, he organized a revolutionary society, Friends of the Liberty of the Press, which, progressing beyond its original purpose, set up a plot for the overthrow of the government. The plot was discovered and nine members arrested, but the royalists dared not touch the hero of the galleries. Not only in the Assembly, but on the streets he was applauded by crowds. Wherever he went he was the center of attention, a standard-bearer for liberal thought. He seemed once again endowed with the fervor of 1789, and he was in truth reliving, and once more exulting, in the experience of being at the very heart of where the action was. His eleventh grandchild was born at this time, who, he wrote Jefferson, "has, in addition to the family name of Gilbert, the friendly name of Thomas." He added, "He is born to freedom—born to freedom! The cause of French, of European liberty is far from being lost. If the French people have deplorably erred in the means, they have steadily persevered in the primary object of the revolution."

After the downfall of the Friends of the Liberty of the Press, he joined the *Charbonnerie* (literally, the coal yard), an international secret society. It had been born in the forests of Italy where patriots, plotting against a despotic regime, earned their living by making charcoal. As the membership crossed national boundaries, the society's purpose was enlarged to include the overthrow of tyrants everywhere. Lafayette became the leader of the French cell and built the scanty membership up to forty thousand. At that point the Charbonnerie picked up the plot to overthrow Louis XVIII's government hatched by the Friends of Liberty of the Press. But on Christmas Eve, 1819, when the plot was to be sprung, it was discovered. Lafayette took refuge in the American Legation, from which he tried, without success, to free fellow conspirators who had been arrested. Several of them paid with their lives, but proof of Lafayette's involvement was insufficient to convict a man of his political popularity. As far as the incident itself was concerned, he had a tight alibi. At the hour on Christmas Eve when the coup was supposed to have been pulled off, he had been at Adrienne's grave, where he had spent every anniversary of her death.

After this second plot, the silencing of Lafayette became a primary objective of Louis and his cohorts and Fouché. They tried hard to defeat him in the elections of 1822, but he won in spite of them. Not long after, however, he obliged them by walking out of the Assembly. One of his fellow members of the Charbonnerie was expelled from the Chamber for what was denounced by the royalists as a "seditious" speech. Paying no attention, the member took his seat the next day as usual. A section of the National Guard was called in to remove him. When the troops marched down the aisle, Lafayette ordered the officer in charge to march them out again. The officer hesitated, but not the men. They immediately faced about, obeying the man whose name had become a legend among them. Next the police were sent for. They had no qualms about obeying the Assembly's orders. As they hauled out the protesting member, Lafayette followed them. Sixty other deputies followed Lafayette. "The scene was worthy of the early days of the Revolution," Lafayette later recorded.

He never returned to the Assembly of Louis XVIII, though he ran once more for election. He lost because the royalists had seen to it that the vote would be weighted against the champions of the people. They had passed legislation which apportioned votes according to land ownership and wealth.

The better off an individual was, the more votes he was entitled to cast. The likes of Lafayette had little chance in an election so rigged.

He was neither surprised nor dismayed by the defeat. He considered the triumph of the right wing temporary, for he could see at work, not only in France, but everywhere in Europe, the ferment of freedom. "I am sanguine," he wrote Jefferson. "Notwithstanding the present appearances, the true doctrines have made great progress. There are axioms at which you and I have seen philosophers and patriots stare, not thirty years ago, and which are now commonplace sayings."

During this same period, he had a long and argumentative correspondence with Jefferson over the Missouri Compromise, which was written into law in the United States in 1820, after a yearlong debate in Congress and the nation. The question at issue was whether the sixty-six thousand people of that portion of the Louisiana Purchase which applied to enter the union as the state of Missouri were to be allowed to keep their ten thousand slaves. Naturally, proslavery forces wished to have the *status quo* maintained, while the growing number of abolitionists wanted statehood to be conditional on banning slave ownership. The controversy was settled by allowing Missouri to keep slavery, but prohibiting it in the rest of the purchase above the 36° 30′ north latitude, while at the same time permitting territory split off from Massachusetts to enter the union as the State of Maine, with an antislavery clause in the state constitution. The compromise preserved an even balance between the number of free and slave states, and thus an even balance of pro- and antislavery legislators in the Senate.

Lafayette, who had joined an English antislavery society called Friends of the Negro, as well as the New York Emancipation Society in the United States, and had worked to get black representation for French black colonies in the Assem-

bly, considered the Missouri compromise as a step backward
in America. In an effort to convince him of its wisdom, Jefferson argued that "Spreading the slaves over a larger surface
will dilute the evil everywhere, not add one thing to that unfortunate condition . . . and increase the happiness of those
existing." Lafayette remained unconvinced. He replied:

> The more I think of it, the less I am in agreement. This
> wide blot on American philanthropy is ever thrown in my
> face when I indulge my patriotism in econiums, otherwise
> indisputable . . . Negro slavery raises a sigh or a blush,
> according to the company, American or foreign, where I
> happen to be.

In a subsequent letter, he added:

> Are you sure, my dear friend, that extending the principle
> of slavery to the new raised states is a method to facilitate
> the means of getting rid of it? I would have thought that
> by spreading the prejudices, thought, habits and calcula-
> tions of planters over a larger surface, you would rather
> encrease [*sic.*] the difficulties of final liberation.

The two old friends could differ amicably—and they did.
Others of Lafayette's American friends agreed with him. John
Adams broke the silence of his retirement in his Quincy,
Massachusetts farmhouse to call the compromise "The title
page of a great tragic drama." And even Jefferson, while defending the solution to the problem, called the situation
which spawned it "a fireball in the night."

Despite Lafayette's disapproval, the Missouri Compromise
did nothing to dull his enthusiasm for his second country, or
his longing to revisit American shores. When, at a most op-
portune time, after his defeat in the French elections of 1824,
he received an invitation from the United States Congress to
tour the country, he was delighted. The Congressional invita-

tion was backed by outstanding American patriots, foremost among them Jefferson, Adams and Madison. Congress offered to put a ship at Lafayette's disposal, but this he courteously declined. He embarked in July with his son, Georges, in a private vessel. Admirers organized a parade to bid him farewell, but the government called in troops to break it up. The royalists were delighted with his departure, but they had reached the point of stifling every public demonstration that could be construed as supporting revolutionary goals.

"The Bourbons dig their own grave," Lafayette remarked to his son as they mounted the gangplank. He was undisturbed. At sixty-seven, after forty-three years of experience in political struggles, he was less easily provoked by the present, more perceptive of future possibilities. He looked forward to the sojourn in the country of his heart. It would refresh him for the work at home which he felt lay inevitably ahead.

# 7

---

# *Again the Hero*

LAFAYETTE'S welcome in America was as rousing as his departure from France was cheerless. During a four-hundred-day, five-thousand-mile tour through the States, from August, 1824, to September, 1825, the enthusiasm with which he was received never let up.

Arriving in New York's harbor on a Saturday afternoon, he was greeted with artillery salutes and escorted to the summer house on Staten Island of Daniel Tompkins, Vice-President of the United States. Sunday morning, deputations of citizens from the city flooded the vice-presidential mansion. At dawn Monday morning, pealing bells and roaring cannon ushered in a round of celebrations. Places of business closed for the day. Before noon, nearly fifty thousand spectators had assembled at the Battery, on the southern tip of Manhattan, New York, where Lafayette was supposed to land. At one o'clock he and Georges left Staten Island aboard the steamship *Chancellor Livingston,* the first such vessel he had ever seen. Four more steamships preceded his. The *Cadmus,* on which he had sailed across the Atlantic, followed, towed by two other steamships. Each was loaded with dignitaries, aflutter with flags and blaring with bands. From all the harbor islands salutes were fired as the cavalcade sailed by.

Lafayette disembarked at the Battery at 2:00 P.M. His destination was City Hall, only a few blocks north. But so dense were the crowds en route, and so intense their desire to press close to his barouche, that the drive took two hours.

A band from West Point followed him, playing the "Marseillaise" which he hadn't heard since the return of Louis to the French throne. Veterans of the American Revolution marched on either side of him, wearing ribbons with his portrait and the words "Welcome, Lafayette." Spectators threw flowers in such profusion that he sat waist deep in bouquets. And in spite of efforts of the militia to restrain the burgeoning onlookers, enthusiasts continually broke through the lines to pay their personal tributes.

Lafayette bowed, smiled, waved, reached out to shake hands, and at one point, wept. Adulation had been his before in the mercurial ups and downs of his career, but never before had he experienced such heartfelt spontaneity. Even Le Vasseur, the young man who accompanied him as secretary, and to whom we owe much of the detailed record of his triumphal tour, was dumbfounded. "No king could command such veneration," he recorded. "Only the hearts of free men could produce it."

When Lafayette finally arrived at City Hall, he was greeted by the Mayor:

> General, the posterity of . . . your contemporaries in arms
> . . . will never forget that you came to us in the darkest
> period of our struggle, that you linked your fortune with
> ours, when it seemed almost hopeless, that you shared in
> the dangers, privations and sufferings of that bitter struggle,
> nor quitted until it was consummated on the glorious field
> of Yorktown. Half a century has elapsed since that great
> event and in that time your name has been inseparably con-
> nected with the cause of freedom in the old as in the new
> world.
> The people of the United States look up to you as one of

their most honored parents; the country cherishes you as one of the most beloved sons . . . In behalf of my fellow citizens of New York, and speaking the warm and universal sentiments of the whole people of the United States, I repeat their welcome to our common country.

Lafayette replied:

You have been pleased, Sir, to allude to the happiest times, the unalloyed enjoyments of my public life. It is the pride of my heart to have been one of the earliest sons of America . . . I beg you, Mr. Mayor, I beg you gentlemen, to accept yourselves, and to transmit to the citizens of New York, the homage of my profound and everlasting gratitude, devotion and respect.

The Battery reception, and City Hall greeting were only the beginning of New York's welcome celebration. Every day of his stay, there was a visit to be made, visitors to be received, receptions and military reviews to attend. Every night some dinner was scheduled in his honor. By night, the city was illuminated with sky rockets; by day, guns from the harbor alternated with firecrackers in the streets.

One of the visits most stimulating to Lafayette was with students in the Mulberry Street Schools of the New York Emancipation Society to which he belonged. The schools were maintained for children of escaped slaves who had made their way north. After spending a morning in the classroom, Lafayette told the schools' director that these were "the best disciplined and most interesting schools of children that I have ever seen." Obviously it didn't occur to him to ask why the children needed separate schools of their own. His bows as he accepted flowers from them might well be considered condescending today. So would his ideas about educating slaves for freedom before granting it. But at the time when he made his American tour, his attitudes were considered radical by all except abolitionists.

Everywhere his presence was in demand. Would he speak at this society? Would he dedicate that memorial? Would he lay the cornerstone for another new building? Lafayette was prepared to accept all invitations and poor Le Vasseur had a deal of trouble keeping the calendar straight. "You cannot, sir," he said firmly one day, "not even you, you cannot be in two places at the same hour on the same day."

One of the cornerstone layings was for the Brooklyn, New York, public library. The American poet, Walt Whitman, then only a six-year-old child, was present and was so impressed that sixty years later he remembered the event. "He arrived on a sunny morning in an open, canary-colored barouche," Whitman recalled. "He was not a handsome man as I expected him to be, but he was a commanding figure. He lifted us children up to a safe spot above the excavation, where we could see the ceremony. He kissed me as he set me down."

From New York, Lafayette's itinerary led to Massachusetts. As was the case wherever he went, each part of the country was determined to outdo the welcome extended by others. New England, in particular, as the birthplace of the American Revolution, was bent on excelling New York. When he arrived in Boston to attend a gala dinner on Boston Commons, he was greeted by two hundred girls dressed in white and wearing sashes inscribed *Nous vous aimons, Lafayette* (We love you, Lafayette).

At Harvard, where son Georges received an honorary degree, he spoke to a gathering of students and faculty, calling the university "a striking example of . . . contributions that can be made to promote the progress of civilization and learning." After addressing the Massachusetts Senate, he was congratulated on his command of the English language. Bowing, but with a bit of twinkle in his eye, he replied, "Why should I not speak easily, being an American just returned from a long visit to Europe?" Before leaving Boston, he and Georges called on the Perkins family who had arranged Georges's stay in America while Lafayette was in prison.

From Boston he returned to New York to keep an engagement for his sixty-seventh birthday party, held by the Society of the Cincinnati. The Society, an organization of the veterans of the American Revolution, had been founded in 1781, with membership open to the French as well as the American veterans. It was named for a fifth century B.C. Roman farmer who left his fields to serve his country as consul and as general, and after defeating invading tribesmen, returned to his farm, refusing further public life. The parallel with the farm recruits who made up so much of the revolutionary forces and with George Washington, who became the Society's first president, is obvious.

Lafayette cherished the gold and enamel medal which was the emblem of the Society and when formally dressed, always wore it in a position of honor above his other decorations. At his birthday ball, Lafayette, dressed in white satin, with the gold medal glimmering on his chest and the golden hilt of the sword presented to him forty-five years ago by the Continental Congress gleaming at his side, was the center of attraction. He discarded his cane to dance a few times with the wives of dignitaries. Then, in greater demand than he could meet, he asked his son to share the honors with him. Le Vasseur delightedly took over dignitaries' daughters and other younger guests. One wonders whether there flashed through Lafayette's mind the memory of a ball a half century earlier, at which the French court, rippling with echoes of Marie Antoinette's contemptuous laughter, had mocked the quadrille steps of a seventeen-year-old.

At two o'clock in the morning, Lafayette left the dancers to take a steamer engaged to sail him up the Hudson to Albany where he was due the following day. His itinerary was kaleidoscopic: after Albany, Trenton; after Trenton, Philadelphia. In Trenton, twenty-four girls, dressed to represent the twenty-four states of the Union, greeted him. "Except in your Congress," said Lafayette in reply to their greeting, "your states were never before so well represented." In Philadelphia, where he had a week's stopover, there were daily parades, daily receptions in the hall where the Declaration of Independence had been signed, and every night a banquet. His right hand became so swollen from shaking hands with thousands, that he was forced to shake with his left instead.

From Philadelphia he went on to Washington for the first visit to the capital city. Here he met Andrew Jackson, then Senator from Tennessee, who was to be added to his list of close American friends. When the two were introduced, Jackson recalled having seen Lafayette at one of the fetes with which Charleston had celebrated the arrival of the French volunteer. Only ten at the time, Jackson had nevertheless retained a sharp memory of Lafayette's enthusiasm. "It has not failed," Lafayette assured him, "though time has tempered my vision of the immediately possible."

Congress made much of him. He was received in the Senate and in the House of Representatives. So great was the uproar in the Senate that the chair adjourned the session to permit senators to crowd around him. The House, with every branch of government represented in the galleries, extended the official welcome of the nation. "General, you are in the midst of posterity," said Henry Clay, the house speaker.

"No, Mr. Speaker," Lafayette replied, "posterity has not yet begun for me, since in the sons of my companions and friends, I find the same public feelings on my behalf which I have had the happiness to experience in their fathers." He added: "In this august place I have, Sir, the pleasure to contemplate not only that Constitutional Union so necessary to these states . . . but also a great political school which other parts of the world may attentively observe, and so be taught the practical science of true social order."

In contrast with his Congressional welcome was the aloofness of the French Ambassador to the United States. Instructed by Louis to ignore Lafayette's visit, the Ambassador refused an invitation to attend the ceremonies in the House. When Clay, wanting to make sure Lafayette didn't think the Ambassador had not been invited, diplomatically mentioned that he must have been detained, Lafayette replied, "I did not come to America to meet my own countrymen." He was neither surprised nor disturbed.

What truly delighted him was the lack of pomp in the American government, particularly the simplicity of life in the White House. Immediately he contrasted that atmosphere with the airs he had always loathed in European courts. "No sentries, no guards, no valets, no adornments," he commented. "None of the puerile fantasies for which so many ninnies dance attendance in the antechambers of the palaces of Europe."

At his request, he was taken to Mount Vernon. His son, Georges, Washington's stepson's son, George Washington Custis, and Le Vasseur accompanied him to Washington's grave, an above-ground sarcophagus, though not the elaborate family mausoleum built seven years later. Thoughtfully, Custis drew the others aside, leaving Lafayette alone. After some time, Lafayette rejoined them. "He was a great statesman, I believe," said Le Vasseur. "Yes," replied Lafayette, and then to Custis, "he was the father of us both." Custis drew from his pocket a ring which he gave to Lafayette as a token, he said, "of continuing family friendship." As Lafayette slipped it on his finger, Custis added, "Where liberty dwells, there must be the country of Lafayette."

From Mount Vernon Lafayette journeyed to Monticello, accompanied by James Madison. There the two spent four days with the eighty-one-year-old Jefferson, conversing from morning to night. Again and again, Lafayette brought the conversation around to the subject of slavery. That was, to his mind "the one blot on the free but responsible society" which the American Constitution had established. Wherever he had a suitable platform, he raised objections to the blot. "It is incredible," he said in one speech in Washington, "that a people who have shed so much blood for their own independence should deny the same way of life to another people." He warned, in phrases that foreshadowed the words of Abraham Lincoln, "Do you not realize the issue at stake is not merely their freedom, but ours? Freedom cannot be restricted. It is for all or for none."

By February he grew restless with the ritual of the Capital. He wrote to his daughters at La Grange, "I move among brilliant gatherings and touching, but I must constantly give myself over to them." He decided to leave Washington for rural areas where he might have more contact with ordinary people. One of his early stops was a town named for him, Fayetteville, North Carolina. He soon discovered that a third of Fayetteville's population of four thousand were slaves who tended the area's lucrative tobacco crops. Despite the turnout wherever he was taken he found the visit depressing. He looked for a suitable occasion to raise the issue of that "one blot" on American freedom which so depressed him. His opportunity came when the Mayor, introducing him at a rally said, "The sun of liberty is everywhere extending the sphere of its creating influence . . . The thrones of Europe, which have no support but the power of bayonets, have been shaken to their foundations and the genius of our country may speedily celebrate the spirit of universal emancipation."

"Let us pray," Lafayette replied, "that the citizens of Fayetteville may as speedily celebrate that spirit of universal emancipation." Le Vasseur noted that Lafayette's irony was lost on the townspeople and their officials. "If the several hundred slaves brought in from the fields understood," he added, "no doubt they dared not manifest their feelings for their faces were impassive throughout."

From Fayetteville, Lafayette moved on through both Carolinas, through Georgia, Louisiana, Mississippi, Missouri, Illinois, then southward again to Tennessee, where, in Nashville, Andrew Jackson met him. The crowd awaiting his arrival drew back and let Jackson step forward alone to greet him. In the front line of spectators stood some forty veterans of the American Revolution, with each of whom Lafayette paused to exchange a few words. One he embraced. He was a Frenchman who had fought several times with Lafayette and who had become a naturalized American citizen.

Jackson took his guest to his estate, The Hermitage. There the two men talked far into several nights. One evening Jackson showed Lafayette a pair of handsomely chased silver dueling pistols. "Do you recognize them?" Jackson asked.

"Yes," replied Lafayette, "they are the ones I gave General Washington in 1788."

"He gave them to me in 1796 when I was elected to the House of Representatives from Tennessee," Jackson explained. "I had helped prepare the State Constitution."

"I feel real satisfaction in finding them in the hands of a man so worthy of the heritage," Lafayette said.*

The two men were an unlikely pair to hit it off so well: Jackson, a lanky frontiersman, earthy in dress, crude in speech, and Lafayette, the polished country gentleman, fastidious and suave. But externals were not what drew them together: rather they found common ground in shared convictions. Both men believed in the collective wisdom of the people and the necessity for maintaining channels through which that wisdom could work. Both had served the United States with distinction as military men and as negotiators abroad. "Old Hickory," as Jackson was known, was a presi-

* The pistols were willed by Jackson to Georges Washington Lafayette. They are now in a small museum at Chavaniac.

dential candidate at the time of his conversations with Lafayette. Lafayette agreed with every plank in his platform, though he wished that a stand against slavery had been included. He recognized that Jackson was typical of a new breed of leadership in America, emerging as the country's borders ballooned westward. In the course of his western tour Lafayette met a good sampling of these "men with their bark on," as they were called, and he was impressed with their determination and passion for direct action. "These are the thriving offspring of the American Revolution," he told Le Vasseur. "Their vigor equals that of their progenitors. Their character is different because the times are different. My generation of Americans founded a republic. This generation must secure and expand it."

He was fascinated with the state of Ohio, which he reached via the Ohio and Mississippi Rivers. In the Ohio, the *Natchez,* which had been hired for him, struck a snag, ripped her bottom and sank. With her sank some six hundred as yet unanswered fan letters Americans had addressed to Lafayette. Le Vasseur, already overburdened with correspondence, confessed that he found this accident no great tragedy, there being no other losses. The party reached shore safely in a lifeboat and were transferred to another ship, the *Paragon,* which landed in Cincinnati where General William Henry Harrison waited for Lafayette. Harrison, another of the men with their bark on, like Jackson, would one day be President of the United States. After a round of entertainment in Cincinnati, Lafayette declared it to be "the most cultured city of the West. . . . Ohio," he said, "should be listed as one of the wonders of the world."

From Cincinnati he traveled northeast, visiting in Vermont and New Hampshire, and meeting once again in upper New York State with Indian tribes. The Oneida chief with whom he had negotiated during the American Revolution, now aging like Lafayette, came to see "Kayewla." As they smoked

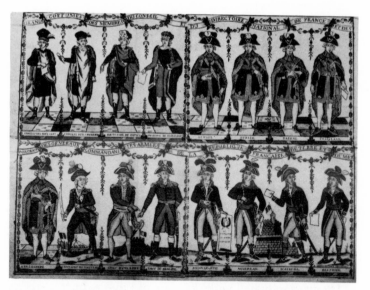

The Rotten Bellies. The members of the Directory and their generals. *Courtesy of the French Embassy Press and Information Division.*

Madame de Lafayette and her daughters join Lafayette in prison at Olmütz. *Courtesy of the New York Public Library.*

Lafayette at the time of
his retirement to La Grange.
*Courtesy of the Lafayette
Memorial Foundation.*

La Grange. *Courtesy of the Lafayette College Library.*

Street fighting during the Revolution of 1830. *Photograph by Pierre Dubure, courtesy of the French Embassy Press and Information Division.*

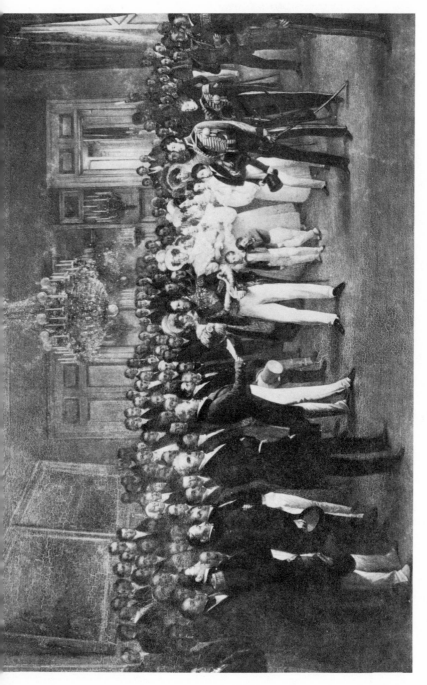

Louis Philip being read the declaration of the Deputies limiting his power. *Courtesy of the New York Public Library.*

A celebration in Paris of the centennial of Lafayette's death.
*Courtesy of the Commissariat Général au Tourisme, Service de Documentation et de Propagande.*

A recreation of Lafayette's embarcation on *La Victoire* for the French celebration of the bicentennial of his birth in 1957. *Courtesy of the French Embassy Press and Information Division.*

the peace pipe together, the chief reached out his hand to touch Lafayette's still red hair. To cover the line where it receded from his forehead, Lafayette combed his hair forward. When the chief pointed to his own bald pate and shook his head, Lafayette lifted the covering locks to expose his bare spot. The two men broke into laughter.

By June 17th, Lafayette was back in Boston to take part in the celebration of the fiftieth anniversary of the Battle of Bunker Hill. He was the central figure in a parade of seven thousand veterans, active troops and members of civic organizations which wound its way to the hill between lines of some two hundred thousand wildly cheering and waving citizens. He was introduced by Daniel Webster, a brilliant lawyer who was then a member of Congress. Spellbinding as an orator, Webster made what is ranked as one of his four most moving speeches in presenting Lafayette to fellow Bostonians.*

"Through Lafayette," Webster wound up, "heaven saw fit to ordain that the electric spark of liberty should be conducted from the New World to the old." Lafayette then laid the cornerstone of the monument which still marks the battle site. That evening a dinner was held for him in army barracks. He told his audience of some four thousand soldiers that, "As this is the fiftieth anniversary of the freedom of America, so after another fifty years we shall hold a jubilee to celebrate an emancipated Europe." Throughout the trip, his joy in the progress of America was ever a reminder to him of all that remained to be done in the old world.

After Boston he once again visited with Jefferson, Madison and Monroe, and accepted from the newly elected President, John Quincy Adams, an invitation to celebrate his sixty-

* The other three are a second Bunker Hill address in 1843, a previous speech in Plymouth of the occasion of the two hundredth anniversary of the landing of the Pilgrims, and a eulogy in 1826 on the same-day deaths of Thomas Jefferson and John Adams.

eighth birthday on September 6th in the White House. At dinner that night, raising his glass in a toast to Lafayette, Adams hailed him and George Washington in the same breath, speaking of their birthdays as far apart, but their hearts as one. The gesture was precedent-breaking, this being the first time a toast had ever been proposed in the White House to a foreigner. Not as a foreigner, however, did Americans regard Lafayette; they had welcomed him home as their own.

France, on his return, gave him a shocking contrast with the sprawling, vigorous republic through which he had been traveling for the last year. Louis XVIII had died. He had been succeeded by his brother, Charles, Count d'Artois, who became Charles X. Charles was a throwback to pre-Revolutionary, indeed almost to feudal, times. He had reduced the amounts for which government bonds could be redeemed, using the funds thus freed to pay emigrés for their losses during the revolution. He had surrounded himself with arch-royalist ministers. He had muzzled the press which resorted to printing what they pleased in Belgium and smuggling their uncensored papers over the border into France. As one journalist commented, "He might as well have presented a bill declaring that printing is abolished in France to the profit of Belgium."

Secret societies sprang up in opposition to the regime. *Aide-toi, le ciel t'aidera* (Help yourself and heaven will help you) was the most active of these underground groups in which journalists who objected to censorship, bankers who objected to the depreciation of bonds, and working men who objected to Charles's efforts to restrict voting rights to superwealthy landowners all mingled together. The historian, François Chateaubriand, a member of Aide-toi, remarked, "Yet another government hurling itself down from the towers of Notre Dame." He was referring to an attempt by Charles to restore the divine rights of kings and the partnership of state and church. Subsequently, Charles would go to the extreme of proposing that theft from churches be punishable by beheading.

Confronted with this political climate, Lafayette characteristically went into action. He ran successfully for election in the Chamber of Deputies. Not long afterward, Charles dissolved the Chamber, leaving the House of Peers to remain as a puppet parliament to rubberstamp his edicts. The people promptly reelected the entire group of deputies. Charles redissolved it. The issue was drawn.

On July 27th, the people of Paris resurrected a tradition established in the Revolution. They took to the streets in protest. Charles ordered troops to disperse them. The Parisians built barricades and fought with whatever came to hand; brooms, dishes, saucepans, shoes, scale weights, flower pots, bedposts. Foremost among the street fighters were students from one of the nation's most distinguished schools, L'École Polytechnique. Joined by ranks of workmen, they climbed the towers of Notre Dame, there to unfurl the tricolor. From Notre Dame they surged to City Hall, leading a charge which put the city government in the hands of the protesters. The king's troops retired in confusion.

Then came the cry for Lafayette. The students and their allies had routed the king's cohorts in three days of the kind of street-to-street battling in which Parisians had become adept. Now they were in charge. How to restore order? How to govern? Lafayette had brought peace to Paris before; would he do it again? The victors wanted to dispense with the monarchy and make Lafayette the first president of a French republic.

Lafayette took over and he restored order, but he made no promises about the presidency. He said merely that if and when the Chamber of Deputies constitutionally approved such a change in government, he would consider the offer. The Chamber approved the change with remarkable rapidity by working through the night. Lafayette was face-to-face with decision. His was the opportunity to become the George Washington of France. Should he seize it?

For the man who had endeavored for the greater part of his life to establish representative government in his country, the opportunity to head the first such was tempting, but conflicting with the temptation was his lifelong philosophy of government for France. Despite his advocacy for America of a republic with executive power vested in the presidency— as a Frenchman he remained a strong constitutional monarchist. Had there been no candidate for the throne other than Charles, the date of the country's transformation to an enduring republic might not have been postponed for forty-five years. But that was not the way the chips of history fell. A new candidate was already approaching Paris.

In the meanwhile, Charles, his back to the palace wall, sent Lafayette a message that he was prepared to revoke the ordinances which had triggered the rebellion, dismiss the hated royalist ministers and recognize the people's choice in the Chamber of Deputies. As strongly opposed to an absolute king as he was in favor of a constitutional one, and with no faith whatsoever in Charles, Lafayette replied unhesitatingly: "It is too late. Reconciliation is impossible. You have ceased to reign."

Receiving the note, Charles recognized defeat. "I know but two men who have ever stood for the same principles," he said, "myself and Monsieur de Lafayette. He as the defender of liberty and I as the king of aristocracy." He fled and shortly afterward, abdicated.

Hoping to succeed him, the next candidate for the throne of France rode into Paris. He was Louis Philippe, Duke d'Orléans, son of the Orléans who had pretended to side with the people during the revolution, in the hope of becoming king himself. Orléans's friends called on Lafayette, urging him to support the Duke. Even the American Ambassador, at

President Jackson's request, expressed informally the view that a king who would reign but not govern might be the most temperate means of bringing stable democracy to France.

The political gossip of Paris was that Louis Philippe had persuaded the ambassador to persuade Jackson in his favor, but the rumor seems unlikely, given Jackson's temperament. More likely, Jackson's motive may have been to help Lafayette avoid the turbulence he himself was encountering. The sweeping economic and political reforms which he believed an expanding America required to shift from an agricultural to an industrial society had made him many enemies. He was cartooned as King Andrew I, trampling the Constitution under foot, and at the moment of the French Revolution of July, 1830, he was coping with South Carolina's threat to drop out of the United States. Though Jackson wasn't afraid to defy the United States Congress and disdain decisions of the Supreme Court, he may have felt that Lafayette's France, which had accepted four different kinds of government since its first revolution, lacked the roots to sustain another drastic change. Jackson hints at this motivation in some subsequent correspondence with Lafayette when he says, "Though you and I have like objectives, our countrymen being what they are, we cannot pursue them by the same means."

In any event, Lafayette's own philosophy, reinforced by the opinion of his friend made him a willing listener to the supporters of Louis Philippe. They had no difficulty in winning his assent to their argument that a constitutional monarchy was the right course for France at the time. The only question in Lafayette's mind was the extent to which Louis Philippe, Duke of Orléans, could be relied upon to fill that role. As a safeguard he proposed to the Chamber of Deputies that the duke be offered the crown while at the same time limitations on its power and guarantees of the people's liberty be proclaimed.

On July 30th, Louis Philippe, swathed in the tricolor, headed a horseback procession to City Hall, where Lafayette was waiting for him. Behind the duke rode the deputies. Along the way the crowds were sullen, but not violent. Occasionally there were shouts of "Down with the Bourbons! Long live liberty! Long live a republic!" The assemblage in front of City Hall parted peaceably to let the procession through. Dismounting, Louis Philippe and the Deputies went inside.

Lafayette greeted the Duke, and the declaration of the Deputies, limiting his powers, was read to him. It was long and detailed. As time ticked on, the crowd outside grew restless. People began to gather in ominous knots, buzzing like swarming bees. A guard reported to Lafayette that he sensed trouble. Lafayette nodded and extended his hand to the Duke. "Come with me," he said. Then, seizing a tricolor flag, the man who had saved the French throne from a balcony in Versailles, led Louis Philippe to salvation on the balcony of City Hall. He wrapped the flag around both their shoulders and embraced the king-elect. The people once again responded to the intuitive touch of this defender and symbol of French liberty. He drew from them the necessary cries of approval: "Long live the Duke d'Orléans! Long live Lafayette!" Behind the two symbols the deputies stood en masse. No one noticed that Louis Philippe had made no comment on the reading of the Declaration. He remained as uncommitted as when he had ridden into Paris. "A republican kiss," said Chateaubriand, "has made a king." The next day a newspaper cartoon showed Lafayette handing the duke a crown with the words, "Sire, pray put it on."

Obviously the duke had to maintain the support of the man responsible for the throne. Instead of summoning Lafayette, he went to see him. The talk naturally turned on the manner in which France was to be governed. Lafayette began the conversation. "You know, of course, that I, as a republican, look upon the Constitution of the United States as the best ever devised."

"Exactly," said Louis Philippe, "but do you think we in France could adopt it as it stands?"

"No indeed," answered Lafayette. "What we need here today is a popular throne, entirely surrounded by republican institutions." "That is just what I think myself," said the duke and Lafayette believed him. A few days later he was installed on the throne.

The people had accepted the new king in the wave of emotion which Lafayette had induced, but their alertness had not been dulled by the melodrama. When the excitement died down, their critical senses, sharpened by forty-one years of national upheaval in one form or another, surfaced, and with them a series of crises.

The first was touched off by the trial of the hated ministers of the abdicated Charles X. On charges of violation of the constitution, they were tried in the Luxembourg Palace in December. Lafayette was well aware that a verdict of not guilty might incite an uprising. He hoped to prevent trouble by appealing directly to the people, but the terrified ministers were demanding the protection of troops and the new king's Minister of the Interior insisted that Lafayette, to whom the king had restored command of the National Guard, provide that protection. Lafayette yielded to him, but warned. "You are using too much of the army and not enough of the people." In front of the Palace, along the left bank of the Seine, the crowds grew larger every day. On the day the verdict was supposed to be announced, immense numbers waited to hear it.

Lafayette moved among them urging restraint, but his cautions fell on deaf ears. The writer, Victor Hugo, who was present, recorded that Lafayette was at one point seized, hoisted to the shoulders of a couple of men and carried about for several minutes, his captors shouting, "Here is General

Lafayette, who wants him?" Lafayette refused to become ruffled, preserving the same calm he had shown when he was
fired at point blank in the mob action on the Champ de
Mars in 1791. He was deposited, unharmed, when an an-
nouncement was made from the palace steps that the verdict
would be delayed for another day. The crowd dispersed in
the dusk.

The next morning they reassembled. A rumor started that
the prisoners had been condemned to death. While the mob,
hopeful but distrusting, sought to verify the story, the Minister of the Interior hurried the prisoners from the back door
of the palace to the fortress of Vincennes where they were to
be confined. The Minister was supposed to turn the prisoners
over to the National Guard, but he had no faith in either the
guards or their commander—"that man with the strange belief that one can reason with the populace," as he described
Lafayette.

When the minister's trick was discovered, the mob started
to charge. Thirty thousand guardsmen presented their bayonets to halt the surge while Lafayette harangued the angry
citizens. Night had fallen and he could see the faces of his
audience only by the light of the torches many carried. On
and on he talked, until in the flickering flares he watched
their faces relax and they quieted, finally attentive to his
pleas for reason.

He was not, however, deceived into believing that he had
brought any permanent peace to the city. He called into a
late night conference the leaders of the Polytechnique youth
who had led the July revolution. "You have helped to de-
throne a king," he reminded them. "Will you now complete
the revolution which you have started by maintaining order?"
The next day, the 22nd of December, masses of students
tramped through Paris wearing sashes on which were printed
the words, *Order Publique.* Behind them tramped thousands
of working men. As they paraded they plastered the city with

placards which read: "The King, elected by us, and Lafayette . . . our friends and yours, have promised on their honor to work for the complete organization of that liberty . . . which we have paid for in July." The procession ended up at the Palais Royal where the king was living. He received the marchers with soothing words. That danger of violence was, for the moment, over.

Louis Philippe was no fool. He recognized as well as Lafayette that he ruled a volatile people. But unlike Lafayette, he had no vision of their capabilities. The man who had made him king had done so in order to give the people room to develop their nation. The king he had made sought to manipulate the people to his own advantage.

To woo them he strolled about the streets like any ordinary citizen, unaccompanied by guards or courtiers. Whenever idlers gathered outside his residence, he brought his family onto a balcony, waved the tricolor and sang the "Marsaillaise"—a hollow imitation of Lafayette's tactics. To these gestures he soon added bribery and corruption of deputies and the bourgeois business class which was becoming the most powerful bloc of the country's voters. Technically he remained a constitutional monarch; there was no stamping on freedom of the press or of expression, for example, no attempt to dissolve the Chamber. Rather than breaking the law, he subverted it. That subversion would cause further crisis was predictable.

# 8

---

# POSTLUDE
## *Symbol of the Future*

I N the 1830's the people's frustration with Louis Philippe's subtle subversion of their will erupted in a series of crises from Paris to Lyons, the two cities where street fighting was bloodiest. In 1834, simultaneous riots in both cities were quelled only by the brute force of the National Guard which the king had remodeled into an instrument of his will. Contrary to Lafayette's hope for the guard as a "citizen army," in which service would be obligatory, Louis Philippe sold appointments to the sons of bankers who could pay for the necessary equipment and make a contribution to the royal treasury besides. Whereas Lafayette had wanted the guard to represent people, the king made it represent prestige. To the banker and his son, the appointment spelled status.

To one of Louis Philippe's aides-de-camp Lafayette objected, "The only way of insuring peace and quietness in

France is to incorporate in the National Guard every work-man without exception . . . The working men are . . . moral men whose good instincts should be encouraged. They love liberty and understand it." He gave the same message to the king, but the message fell on deaf ears. The royal re-action was, "How ridiculous to arm the people, especially the lower people." Louis Philippe and his coterie regarded Lafayette as a "political fool."

Their refusal to accept the advice of a "fool" who had lived through enough revolutions to know the symptoms, produced precisely the conflict between the people and the militia which Lafayette had hoped to avoid. The Guard be-came a symbol of the new caste system in which men of money replaced nobility and the working man had no place. Although workers made up the majority of the country's citizens, government was as inaccessible to them as ever. It was impossible for them to compete for attention in the Chamber of Deputies which, as one liberal newspaper jibed, "is a great bazaar where everyone barters his conscience for a job." Almost half the deputies moonlighted on profitable government jobs. Those who already had businesses of their own, received grants to expand their facilities. Opportunities for employment were extended to their relatives. If they tangled with the law, the courts were bidden to treat them gently. In return for these rewards, they naturally voted, as they were expected to do, for such legislation as the king favored and against such legislation as he opposed.

Nor had they any need to fear the reaction of their con-stituents. The law restricted the right to vote to those who made enough money to be in the upper half of the tax brackets of the country, and this upper half received the same royal favors as the deputies. The some thirty million whose labor made their financial success possible were hopelessly disenfranchised. Moreover the law applied not only to na-tional elections but even to voting for regional councils and municipal communes. From top to bottom the system was rigged in favor of the well-to-do bourgeois who wanted to be even more so.

The major spokesman for the rights of voteless citizens was the Movement, a group of reformists of which Lafayette was a prominent leader. The voters called themselves the Resistance, meaning resistance to electoral reform. To the far right, surviving royalists opposed both the Movement and the Resistance, while to the far left the street mobs opposed all measures save those for which they themselves chose to clamor. Two or more of these political clusters in the same spot at the same time inevitably added up to riot. The Revolution of 1830 had by no means settled the fate of the country to the satisfaction of any of them.

Nevertheless, Lafayette was philosophical about the eventual outcome. Instead of lamenting the Revolution as a total failure, he sought out, as though with a magnifying glass, those few results which could be used as a base for further progress. "I am not of those who say we gained nothing in the Revolution of July," he said. "I recall juries in . . . political matters, liberty promised in education . . . some legislative and electoral reforms . . ." He did recognize, however, that these improvements represented only inches in a course which must stretch for miles. And so he kept on nudging, urging, beckoning, wherever he could.

He considered the most important goal to be that of the Movement, farsweeping electoral reform, for through it all other reforms might be accomplished. "The right to elect does not come from up above," he insisted. "It belongs to all citizens and no one but those who are incapable of using the right should be excluded. . . . I do not think it is necessary for a Frenchman to be able to pay a tax of two hundred francs in order to acquire the honesty which will keep him immune from selling his vote, nor the good sense which will make him choose a decent representative for his country." In an

address in Meaux, he went on to detail some of the changes
he believed could be achieved by ballot, once universal suffrage became a reality:

> I should like to see in our program religious liberty so long
> as cult is removed from the civil state and consciences from
> the intolerance of believers and unbelievers: free educa-
> tion, so long as the people who receive from the state pri-
> mary instruction are not prevented from having family and
> private education; liberty of the press which must be for-
> ever freed from the present entanglements of printing and
> newspaper taxes . . . lastly abolition of the hereditary
> peerage.

While working toward such goals in France, Lafayette also
found time to champion them in other European nations.
Poland, especially, interested him, and he begged unsuccessfully in the National Assembly for French aid to the Poles
whose country had been occupied by the Russians and who
were desperately trying to throw them out. When the Czar
put down the Polish rebellion, many of the rebels fled to
Paris. They made Lafayette an honorary general of the Polish
National Guard. On the anniversary of their uprising, Lafayette paraded through the streets of Paris with the exiles, wearing the guard uniform with which they had honored him.

Still, his main sights were trained on France and the condition of his compatriots. Mellower by more than half a
century than the teenager who had dashed off to join the
American Revolution, now over twice the age of the indig-
nant commander who had rushed back from Metz to cast the
gauntlet at the Jacobins, Lafayette's focus on events had
shifted. He thought less of the moment, more of the future.
"Though I would like in my lifetime to see the hereditary
peerage abolished," he said, "the fact of the matter is that
the peerage is becoming powerless. The new supporters of
the throne are the men of finance. To their quarter the cen-

ter of power has moved. It is with them, therefore, that the rights of the people remain to be worked out."

He was seeing with stunning clarity the unfinished business of the 1830 Revolution. By supplanting a seedy nobility with a robust, business-minded bourgeoisie as the influential class of the nation, the rebellion had spotlighted the struggle between boss and worker which was the main economic and political drama of the day.

The struggle was the outcome of the transition from an agricultural to an industrial economy, known as the Industrial Revolution. French progress in industrializing had been slow —the Revolution was a century old in England before it began in France. Once started, however, the process rolled with such speed as to create within forty years a twenty-five percent increase in foreign trade, a fifty percent increase in the production of iron and a crisscrossing of the country with eleven thousand miles of railroad track. Prosperity paced production, but remained entrenched at the top. At the bottom were the exploited, underpaid workers. In 1848, they were urged to reverse their position in a *Manifesto* which Karl Marx and Friedrich Engels wrote in Paris. The *Manifesto* advised them to seize and share among themselves ownership of the means of production. Few of the French workers went all the way with Marx and Engels. They were not so much interested in owning the whole pie as in forcing the owners to recompense them with a fair share of it. For this purpose, in which they were supported by students, they fostered the next significant revolution in France, the Revolution of 1848.

As Lafayette had foreseen, the struggle for representative government during the latter half of the nineteenth century lay between the machine operators in blue overalls or smocks, and the investors in frock coats and top hats. The 1848 Revolution deposed a king and installed—briefly—a republic. It was becoming clear that if the top hats wished to maintain profit from their investments in the new industrial scene, they would have to consider also the demands of the men in blue, who were acquiring the power to make or break governments.

Lafayette did not live to help direct the course of the 1848 crisis, but he helped nourish the ideas of a number of others who would join the revolutionists. Every Tuesday, he held a salon in his Paris residence, Rue d'Anjou–Saint Honoré. All day the cobbled courtyard was crowded with carriages. Inside, the long ground floor living room was crowded with some of the most talented members of the French and European vanguard thinkers. Beneath an original engraving of the Declaration of Independence and another of Washington's farewell address, the guests conducted passion-sparked discussions.

The poet, Alphonse Lamartine, who would head the government established by the 1848 Revolution was among the regulars. So too was the novelist-poet-dramatist Victor Hugo who would fight at the barricades in the streets in that Revolution and would live to serve in the National Assembly of France's first fully democratic government, established on Bastille Day, 1785. The Polish born musician, Frédéric Chopin, who, though self-exiled in France, was deeply grateful for Lafayette's espousal of the cause of Polish freedom, was often present. The poet Alfred de Musset, whose just-published *Tales of Italy and Spain* had made an immediate name for him in the literary world, was accompanied by his mistress of the moment, Amandine Aurore Dupin, whose novels were signed, "George Sand." Ideas from the salon made their imprint on her work; her early romantic concern with affairs of the heart later deepened into preoccupation with social reform.

Along with leaders in the French arts came labor leaders and Lafayette's Assembly colleagues, also visitors from America, statesmen, freedom fighters, politicians from Italy, Germany, Poland and Holland, all eager to exchange views with the salon frequenters and especially with the salon's host. As a participant described the attendance:

Friends bring friends, sons their fathers, travelers their companions. All who figure in politics, science, literature, popular causes are crowded together . . . some in dirty boots, some in silk stockings, some in uniform, some in buttoned frock coats . . . Thither the whole of France, the whole of Europe, the whole of America have sent their deputations. Lafayette himself . . . walks among the groups . . . As he comes the groups thin out and make way for him while everybody whispers, "It is he."

As La Grange had been, the Rue d'Anjou–Saint-Honoré became an intellectual capital for men with their minds on tomorrow. Lafayette had always believed that the Revolution in which he had been active could and would serve as examples for nations whose liberation was yet to come. His salon provided a like inspiration. The free and spirited talk was one more contribution to his Bunker Hill vision of "an emancipated Europe."

It was his last contribution. In early May, 1834, he was drenched in one of the spring deluges that green the French summer. He fell ill with pneumonia. Salon regulars who called to inquire about his condition received no good word. His children were summoned. Paris newspapers reported him dead, an incident which amused him. But he had no doubt that he was dying. "Look," he said to the children, "life is a bit like an oil lamp. When there is no more oil—pouf—the flame goes out." On May 20th, as dawn filled the spaces between the slats in shutters drawn across the bedroom windows, he kissed the locket he always wore containing Adrienne's portrait and her lock of hair. The locket slid from his hand, his head turned to one side. There was no more oil.

A month before his death, the king he had crowned had put down the Lyons-Paris riots. Since then all public demonstrations of any sort had been strictly forbidden. Lafayette's funeral was classified as a demonstration. And it might well have turned into one. Louis Philippe may have rightly believed that the burial of the champion of the rights of man and the citizen could, in the climate of that moment, become a touchstone for another uprising.

For whatever reason, all but the simplest of ceremonies was barred. Military rites, publicity, were ruled out. The funeral was sparsely attended, for half Paris thought Lafayette had died the week before; the other half didn't know that he had died at all. Georges Washington, Anastasie and Virginie bound the corners of his coffin with the tricolor. It was carried to the de Noailles family plot in the cemetary of Picpus, not far from a Place de la Bastille obelisk erected to honor the dead in the 1830 revolution. With them the children bore the sword and epaulets their father had worn as Commander of the National Guard. The waiting grave was lined with soil brought from Bunker Hill by an American man-of-war, the *Brandywine*. When the coffin had been lowered it was covered with more American earth.

The history of the Picpus cemetary began in the fifteenth century when a small band of monks living in a shelter there were credited with curing fleabites (*pique-puces*) which were afflicting all Paris. Later, nuns of Saint Augustine acquired the land and built a convent on it. During the Revolution of 1789, the government took over the property and used the convent garden as a mass dump for the bodies of the guillotined. After the Revolution, Adrienne bought the site from the government and leased it for a small sum to the Bernadine nuns. The nuns inscribed the names of those who died in the Reign of Terror on tablets in the chapel and prayed for them constantly. Adrienne herself often went there to pray for her mother, grandmother and sister.

Today the little Picpus cemetary, wedged between a school and a hospital, and ringed with high-rise apartment houses, is hard to find. The entrance, unmarked on the outside, is through a tall, heavy, wooden gate. The gate opens into the courtyard of the Chapel of Saint Augustine, originally given and endowed by Adrienne. On the inner face of the gate is a small plaque, installed by the Daughters of the American Revolution, that informs the visitor who has found his way thus far, that Lafayette lies buried in the cemetary.

One progresses through another gate to the garden which was the body dump of the revolution, but which is now well tended and luxuriantly planted. At the far end of the garden, a third gate opens into the cemetary itself. At the farthest end of the cemetary, bounded by two of its walls and squared off by a grilled iron fence, the graves of Lafayette and Adrienne lie side by side. Centered between them at the head of flat stone markers, an American flag floats from its standard.

The lack of ceremony marking Lafayette's death in France was more than made up for by the observances which followed in the United States. President Andrew Jackson ordered that the flag be hung at half mast for a month, everywhere in the nation. For six months, army and navy officers wore mourning bands on their sleeves. A memorial service included the same high military rites that had been accorded the burial of Lafayette's adopted father, George Washington.

Nor did American gratitude to Lafayette end with these formalities. In 1916, a group of American aviators took it upon themselves to make payment in kind. They volunteered for service in the French Air Force about a year before the United States entered World War I. First known as the Lafayette Escadrille, they were later incorporated into the American forces as the 103rd Fighter Squadron. On July 4, 1917, the squadron formed a procession to the Picpus cemetary, led by the American Ambassador to France. The squadron colonel, speaking, he said, for ten million American soldiers, uttered the phrase which later became historic: "France came to our rescue when we fought for our independence. We have not forgotten it. Lafayette, we are here!"

Further acknowledgment of the American debt to Lafayette took place on the one hundredth anniversary of his death.

In May 1934, the United States Seventy-third Congress sent out to a host of dignitaries, French and American, this engraved invitation:

> The honor of your presence is requested
> at the ceremony in commemoration of the
> One Hundredth Anniversary of the death of
> Gilbert du Motier, Marquis de Lafayette
> to be held in the House of Representatives
> at eleven o'clock, ante-meridian
> May twentieth
> Nineteen thirty-four

A proclamation of the day was signed by President Franklin Delano Roosevelt and Secretary of State Cordell Hull. It requested "the people of the United States to observe the day in schools, churches and other suitable places." And observe they did, from the Church of the Huguenots in Staten Island to the Catholic Cathedral in Washington, D.C.; from the Fortnightly Club of Bethlehem, Pennsylvania to the American Bankers and American Bar Associations. Not only on May 20th, but throughout the year, more than a thousand groups, large and small, from New England to California and Minnesota to Louisiana, staged programs recognizing Lafayette's contribution to American liberty and the cause of liberty in the world. As Secretary of State Hull declared at the opening of a Lafayette Centenary Exhibition in the Maison Française at Rockefeller Center in New York, "He was a citizen of the world because he was a friend of man."

At the joint Congressional session, President Roosevelt opened his address with reflections on the Jackson-Lafayette friendship. "A century ago," he said, "Andrew Jackson, in communicating the melancholy news of Lafayette's death to the Congress of the United States, called it 'afflicting intelligence.' And so it was. It made more than one nation mourn, none more than our own."

In Paris, and in the villages of Lafayette's native Auvergne, the centennial was being simultaneously celebrated. Mayors, wearing around their necks their medallioned chains of office, headed solemn parades. Through narrow, cobbled streets, floats rolled, depicting scenes from Lafayette's life: the preparation of the Declaration of the Rights of Man and the Citizen, the presentation of the tricolor to the Paris Commune, the dogged defense of freedom in the National Assembly, the misery of Olmütz. Men costumed like Lafayette in the uniform of the National Guard rode white horses, while police on motorcycles cleared the way.

Again in 1976, the occasion of the United States' two hundredth birthday evoked the memory of Lafayette and the French contribution to the securing of American independence. France's president, Valéry Giscard d'Estaing, a descendent of Admiral Charles d'Estaing, traveled to the United States to address a joint session of Congress and present a birthday present from the French people. The gift was a show at Mount Vernon of a type in which the French specialize. *Son et Lumière* they call it, drama in sound and light. It replayed the story of George Washington and of Lafayette's relationship to him.

An original engraving of Washington's farewell address, signed by him and sent by his wife Martha to Lafayette was presented to the American Senate by a delegation from the French Senate. The delegation was part of a series of many different kinds of exchanges sponsored by the French and American governments and by private organizations in both countries.

In Paris on the Champ de Mars, where once Lafayette had been shot at and once had ridden his white horse at the head of a triumphant procession, a Franco-American festival was held. At the University of Paris, and along the Champs Elysées, a main avenue of the city, more celebrations took place. And everywhere the name of Lafayette was invoked.

Rightly so, not merely because America was the country of his heart, not even because he was responsible for the French aid without which historians doubt if America could have won the revolution, but because in a political sense the American birthday was also his. The Revolution, which he entered as a boyish adventure, opened his eyes to the awesome function and fruits of liberty in the life of a nation. As his own country wavered back and forth between the autocracy of monarchs and mobs, he held out against both, fighting for a middle way in which the authority of government would grow from the orderly expression of popular will. And though he did not live to see France follow this way, it was he, more than any revolutionist of his generation, who blazed it.

# Bibliography

ADAMS, JOHN QUINCY. *The Life of General Lafayette.* Cornish, Lamport and Company, New York, 1851.

BACHMONT, LOUIS PETIT DE. *Memoires Secrets pour Servir a l'Histoire de la Republique des Lettres.* J. Adamson, London, 1777–1789.

BARBAROUX, C. O. *Voyage du Général Lafayette aux États Unis d'Amérique en 1824.* L'Huiller, Paris, 1824.

BARDOUX, A. *La Jeunesse de Lafayette.* C. Levy, Paris, 1892.

BARDOUX, A. *Les dernières années de Lafayette.* C. Levy, Paris, 1893.

BRANDON, EDGAR EWING. *A Pilgrimage of Liberty.* Lawhead Press, Athens, Ohio, 1944.

BRANDON, EDGAR EWING. *Lafayette, Guest of the Nation,* Oxford Historical Press, Oxford, Ohio, 1865.

*Ceremonies in Commemoration of the 100th Anniversary of Lafayette's Death. Congressional Record,* U.S. 73rd Congress, Second Session, Joint Proceedings, May 20, 1934.

CHINARD, GILBERT, ed. *The Letters of Lafayette and Jefferson.* published simultaneously by Johns Hopkins Press, Baltimore, and Les Belles Lettres, Paris, 1929.

CHINARD, GILBERT, ed. *Lafayette in Virginia.* Johns Hopkins Press, Baltimore, 1928.

CLOQUET, JULES. *Recollections of the Private Life of General Lafayette.* Baldwin and Cradock, London, 1835.

COBBETT, WILLIAM, translator. *The Impeachment of Lafayette Containing His Accusation.* Philadelphia, 1793.

COOPER J. FENIMORE. *Letter to General Lafayette.* Baudry's Foreign Library, Paris, 1881.

*Correspondence of the French Ministers in Commission of Foreign Affairs Report.* American Historical Association. Washington, D.C., 1904.

CRAWFORD, M. MACDERMOT. *Madame de Lafayette and Her Family.* J. Pott and Co., New York, 1907.

DE LA BEDOYÈRE, MICHAEL. *Lafayette a Revolutionary Gentleman.* J. Cape, London, 1933.

*Gazette de France.* Ambassade de France. New York: March, April, May, June, 1976 issues.

GILLARD, JOHN T. *Lafayette, Friend of the Negro.* Journal of Negro History, Vol. XIX, No. 4, October, 1934.

GOTTSCHALK, LOUIS REICHENTHAL. *Franklin and Lafayette.* Institut Français, Washington, 1940.

GOTTSCHALK, LOUIS REICHENTHAL. *Lady-in-Waiting.* Johns Hopkins Press: Baltimore, 1939.

GOTTSCHALK, LOUIS REICHENTHAL. *Lafayette Between the American and French Revolutions.* Chicago University Press: Chicago, 1965.

GOTTSCHALK, LOUIS REICHENTHAL. *The United States and Lafayette.* Occasional Paper #5, Augustana Library Publications: Rock Island, Illinois, 1958.

HUME, EDGAR ERSKINE. *Lafayette and the Society of the Cincinnati.* Johns Hopkins Press: Baltimore, 1934.

LAFAYETTE, MARQUIS DE. *Correspondence Inédite de Lafayette, 1793–1801.* C. Delagrave, Paris, 1930.

LAFAYETTE, MARQUIS DE. *Discours au Corps Municipal de Paris,* Lottin: Paris, 1790.

LAFAYETTE, MARQUIS DE, *Extrait d'un Discours Addressé par M. Le Marquis de Lafayette vers la fin d'Octobre aux Officiers de la Garde Nationale.* Gregoire: Paris, 1789.

LAFAYETTE, MARQUIS DE. *Letters from Prison Magdeburg.* January–June, 1881, Series of *the Magazine of American History,* Vol. 6.

LAFAYETTE, MARQUIS DE. *Letters of Washington and Lafayette. Old South Leaflets,* Vol. 7, No. 6. Boston, 1889.

LAFAYETTE, MARQUIS DE. *Lettre de M. M. LaFayette à l'Assemblée Nationale.* Postillion de la Guerre: Paris, 1792.

LAFAYETTE, MARQUIS DE. *Lettres Inédites du Général Lafayette au Vicompte de Noailles, Ecrites des Camps de l'Armée Américaine durant la Guerre de l'Indépendence des États Unis, 1780–1781.* J. Partop: Paris, 1924.

LAFAYETTE, MARQUIS DE. *Memoirs, Correspondence et manuscrits du Marquis de Lafayette.* Saunders and Ottley: London, 1837.

LAFAYETTE, MARQUIS DE. *The Marquis de Lafayette's Statement of His Own Conduct and Principles.* J. Deighton: London, 1799.

LASTEYRIE DE SAILLANT, MARIE ANTOINETTE VIRGINIE. Louis de Lasteyrie, trans., *Life of Madame Lafayette.* L. Techener: Paris, 1872.

LEE, HENRY, *Lafayette's Son Comes to Boston. Bostonian Society Proceedings:* Boston, 1964.

LE NOTRE, G. *Le Terraine de Picpus.* Librairie Academique, Perrin: Paris, 1928.

LE VASSEUR, AUGUSTE. *Lafayette en Amérique en 1824 et 1825.* Baudowin: Paris, 1829.

MADELIN, LOUIS. *Figures of the Revolution.* Macaulay Co.: New York, 1929.

MAUROIS, ANDRÉ. *Adrienne, ou la Vie de Mme. de Lafayette.* Hachette: Paris, 1961.

*New York Times.* New York, May 17, 1976.

NOLAN, JAMES BENNETT. *Lafayette in America, Day by Day.* Johns Hopkins Press: Baltimore, 1934.

PAUL, GEORGES. *Le Général de Lafayette et ses Rapports avec L'Auvergne,* in *Almanach de Brioude et de son Arrondissement,* Année 44, Brioude, 1964.

PENMAN, JOHN SIMPSON. *Lafayette and Three Revolutions,* The Stratford Company. Boston: 1929.

*Revue d'Auvergne,* Numero spécial, publié à l'occasion du bicentennaire de Lafayette. Imprimerie G. de Bussac, Clermont, Ferrand, 1957.

ROUCHON, ULYSSE. *Au Pays de Lafayette.* L'Imprimerie Jeanne

D'Arc: Puy-en-Velay, 1957.

SICHEL, EDITH HELEN. *The Household of Lafayette*. A Constable and Co.: Westminster, 1897.

*Ship Register of Boston and Charlestown*. National Archives Project, WPA. Washington, D.C., 1942.

*The Massif Central*. Ambassade de France: New York, 1976.

VILLAT, LOUIS. *La Révolution et L'Empire*. Les Assemblées Revolutionaires. Presses Universitaires de France: Paris, 1947.

WHITMAN, WALT. *Lafayette in Brooklyn*. George Smith: New York, 1905.

# INDEX